The Art of Making a California-Style Vaquero Bridle Horse

"After 15 years of working together at the ranch and helping with numerous clinics over those years, I have developed the utmost respect and admiration for Mike's horsemanship and his ability to teach and communicate. This book represents Mike's life work. I am confident it will be of significant value to all levels of horsemen who are interested in equine behavior, the training process including many varying techniques, and the practical application of horsemanship, no matter what your discipline."

~ **Terry Crofoot**
Crofoot Cattle Co., Lubbock TX
2-time Champion, 2-time Reserve Champion
Rancheros Visitadores, One Man - One Horse Competition

"Any equine instructor with minimal knowledge can help a rider change common horsemanship mistakes. However, it is often the small, almost unrecognizable mistakes which cause our major horsemanship problems. Mike Bridges has a unique ability to not only help riders recognize these errors, but to help surpass the problem in the simplest way. His instruction helped fast-track my career and will benefit riders at all levels."

~ **Zane Davis**
National Reined Cow Horse Futurity Champion
National Stock Horse Futurity Champion
Multiple NRCHA Worlds Greatest Horseman Finalist

"Mike has a depth of knowledge and a lifetime of experience and tradition around horses and livestock. His understanding of the hackamore and the process to having a horse straight in the bridle is profound. This book is a testimony to Mike's willingness to share his knowledge and experience and should be read by all that are wishing to advance their horsemanship."

~ **David Stuart**
Horsemanship Clinician
David has held horsemanship courses throughout:
Australia, New Zealand, U.S.A., United Kingdom and Europe, Japan, United Arab Emirates

"Having witnessed the results of 15 years of biannual horsemanship and safety clinics held at the ranch, we believe Mike Bridges is one of the most knowledgeable living masters of the Vaquero style of horsemanship. His understanding of a horse's bio-mechanics and mind are exceptional. The most unique aspect of Mike Bridges though, is his ability to teach interested horsemen how to practically apply his knowledge and experience."

~ **Ray Marxer**
The Matador Cattle Company, Montana

"My success in the show pen, as a weekend Non-Pro/Amateur cutter in Oregon, has been profoundly effected by Mike Bridges. His mastery of the biomechanics of the horse and his methods of gymnasticizing the horse have proven effective in maximizing a horse's potential and keeping them sound. I owe much of my cutting success to his guidance in rider influence, reading cattle and herdwork. His gymnastic methods transformed my horse into a consistent winner at the local and state level marking 71-75. Mike is a master horseman, clinician, and mentor and I am proud to be his student."

~ **Dr. Marci Aplin-Scott, DMD**
COCHA Champion 10,000 Amateur 2010
COCHA 3rd Place Non-Pro 2010
OCHA 3rd Place 5,000 Novice Non-Pro 2010
OCHA 4th Place 15,000 Amateur 2010

There is something very special about a finely-made, talented California vaquero style bridle horse; in watching him certainly, but even more in riding him. Tom McGuane captured this feeling exceptionally well in his book "*SOME HORSES*" when he wrote, "I am particularly interested in the bridle horses of California. Theirs is an ancient art conveyed from the time of Spanish rule and there is a solemn romance about these horses with their swan necks, their Santa Barbara Spanish bridles, their lightning quickness, and the steady whir of the rollers in their bits."

Mike Bridges has been exposed to these bridle horses of California his entire life, and has been making them for well over 50 years. The book you hold in your hands outlines his methods for making such a horse; from starting the colt, making a hackamore horse, into the two-rein, and finally "straight up" in the bridle. He keeps no secrets, but gives the reader a lifetime of knowledge and experience. This is not quick fix advice, nor an easy process, for making such a horse takes many years. It is a building process of one brick layered upon another, often using principles of renaissance classical training, combined with the goal of making the ultimate all around cow horse. Month by month, year by year the horse attains higher and higher levels of forward, strength, balance, lightness, and confidence in doing his many jobs—ultimately trusting his rider completely.

Every horseman or horsewoman will find valuable information in this book, but for those making cow horses the well is very deep, and the water cool. This book is likely to become the definitive work on making traditional California Vaquero Style Bridle Horses. Enjoy!!

~ Bill Berner

The Art of Making a California-Style Vaquero Bridle Horse

by Mike Bridges

The Art of Making a California-Style Vaquero Bridle Horse

by Mike Bridges

Author
Mike Bridges
email: bridges7p@gmail.com
ph: 541-227-8081

Publisher of Second Edition
Eclectic Horseman Communications, Inc.
eclectic-horseman.com
email: emily@eclectic-horseman.com
ph: 303-449-3537

First Edition, 2010
Second Edition, 2025

All rights reserved. No part of this book may be reproduced or transmitted by any form or by any means, electronic or mechanical, including photocopying, recording or by any information storage and retrieval system without written permission from the author; except for the inclusion of a brief quotation in a review.

Copyright © 2025 by Mike Bridges
Softcover: ISBN 979-8-9893547-3-3

Editors: Bill Berner & Jim Reilly
Editorial Assistance: Frank Barnett, Terry Crofoot, Sue Greer, Debbie Haber, George Hardeen
Layout & Design: Sue Greer
Cover Photo: Carol Marshall
Second Edition Conversion: Emily Kitching

DEDICATION

This book is dedicated to all the people who have helped me through the years in the development of my horsemanship and cowmanship skills. From some I learned one or two little things. From others, the influence was long-term and profound.

To a great horseman, mentor and true friend, Frank Barnett of Williston, Florida, a seeker of knowledge who continues to keep the fires burning.

To my wife Jill and my two sons, Roy and Justin, for their love and putting up with the wandering ways of a buckaroo.

Introduction from Ernie Morris

Jaquima to Freno

Hackamore to bit is the English way of saying you are teaching a colt to respond to cues given by pulls on the reins attached to the hackamore, then gradually over time transferring the cues to the bit. The objective is to develop a well-trained bridle horse.

As the colt accepts the beginning education with the hackamore and responds to a high degree, it is then time to advance to another learning step, called the two-rein process. The two-rein set-up includes a bosal with mecáte, and a bit with reins. With a two-rein set-up the hackamore used in the beginning training is replaced with a smaller-sized bosal. A traditional hair rope (mecáte) is used for reins. The mecáte should be approximately the same diameter as the bosal. The horse also carries a bit (freno) with reins attached.

During the two-rein process, the colt receives reining signals from the rider through both the bosal and the bit. At the beginning of the two-rein process, nearly all signals are given through the bosal, and little, if any, signals through the bit. The horse merely carries the bit to become accustomed to it in his mouth. Over time as the horse begins to understand these reining signals and becomes accustomed to the bit, the signals are gradually transferred to the bit. This transfer is done by adjusting the reins so the signals can be changed from bosal to bit. The process of transferring the signals from the bosal to the bit is the basis for the two-rein process. As time permits, the colt will accept the bit and respond with great excellence. If done properly, the two-rein process (transfer from jaquima to freno) takes a lot of time. However, the rewards of having a well-reined horse are worth the time.

Mike Bridges includes in this book photos and descriptions that are the recipe for a bridle horse to get to the highest degree of excellence in performance. Mike has done an outstanding job in putting all of this down for others to learn and enjoy. He has made a great contribution to the horse world. This book should be in every horseman's library.

Ernest Morris

~ *Ernie Morris*
Templeton, California

Acknowledgements

There are a number of people who have contributed their time to the completion of this book. Their efforts have certainly enhanced the contents and format of the book. All of them are dedicated horsemen or horsewomen, not all necessarily of this discipline. I'm proud to call all of them my friends. I would like to know what they know.

Frank Barnett Williston, Florida. A master of his craft, He fixes world class horses from a number of different disciplines. The most knowledgeable horseman I know of.

Bill Berner Bend, Oregon. He is a source of great ideas. I could ride with him every day and it would be an enjoyable learning environment.

Jill Bridges Halfway, Oregon. My wife of 26 years. She has a great eye for the horse's structure and movement. An outstanding work ethic. She has many hours invested in this book. I'm blessed.

Terry Crofoot Slaton, Texas. Always does the right thing. A serious student of the processes of training the horse. He has opened more doors for me than I could ever repay.

Debbie Haber Sonoita, Arizona. An outstanding student! She will make all her teachers look good.

Jim Reilly Carlsbad, California. A long time student of the horse. He is very knowledgeable about classical horsemanship, literature and principles. He always makes me think. I'm fortunate to have Jim as a student and friend.

George Hardeen Window Rock, Arizona. One of the editors of this book. He was with me at the start of this book. Also one of my long-term students. George's perseverance and tenacity, demanding that things be right, has been a huge influence in the outcome of this book.

Karl Phillips Vaccaville, California. He took my hand-written text, deciphered it, and then typed it in correct form, so George could read and understand it. What a brave man!

Sue Greer Condon, Oregon. Another long-time student of mine and of the horse. She helped get the final layout done to go to press.

Note: The pictures in this book were taken by a number of people over a period of several years. Some of the names I have forgotten. The ones I can remember are listed here. I want to thank all of you that took these great pictures. Jill Bridges, Karen Hagan, Martin Keller, Kitty Gratzer, Heather Helifx, Vicky Todd, Carol Marshall, Tammy Miltz-Miller and Marcy Alpin-Scott. Again, please forgive me if I have forgotten anyone.

Table of Contents

Dedication .... *vii*

Introduction from Ernie Morris .... *ix*

Acknowledgments .... *xi*

Table of Contents .... *xiii*

Foreword – Mike Bridges .... *xv*

Introduction – Mike Bridges .... *xvii*

    Chapter 1 – Early Training.. 1

    Chapter 2 – The Hackamore as a Discipline............................... 27

    Chapter 3 – Introducing the Hackamore to the Young Horse ... 43

    Chapter 4 – Development Work in the Hackamore: The Exercises 57

    Chapter 5 – Introducing Cattle Work and Roping..................... 85

    Chapter 6 – Riding With the Snaffle Bit 99

    Chapter 7 – Intermediate Hackamore Work 103

    Chapter 8 – Finish Work in the Hackamore 119

    Chapter 9 – The Two-Rein Bosal – How it Works..................... 123

    Chapter 10 – The Horse's Mouth.. 127

    Chapter 11 – Vaquero–Style Bridle Bits 131

    Chapter 12 – Is My Horse Ready for the Bridling Process?........ 145

    Chapter 13 – Starting the Horse in the Two-Rein 147

    Chapter 14 – Riding the Horse Straight in the Bridle 161

    Chapter 15 – Polishing the Stone.. 169

Glossary 175

Expanded Table of Contents... 179

About the Author 185

Foreword

In the following pages, we will explore the development of the California-Style Vaquero Bridle Horse. This exquisite style of horsemanship was developed in Mexico and spread into what is now California over the past 450 years. It's purpose was, and remains, specifically for managing the huge herds of cattle with the greatest amount of efficiency and grace. Long before gold and silicon, the Western economy was based on cattle and remained that way for approximately 270 years.

Within only the last 130 years, however, this horsemanship spread to Oregon, Nevada, Idaho and other places throughout the western United States. More recently, it has begun to move around the world.

It all started with the arrival of the Conquistadors in the 1500s in the form of the warhorse brought from Spain. After subjugating the native people, and with the development of the Catholic missions, cattle began to play a major role in the economics of California. The warhorse was changed into a cattle working horse. This didn't happen overnight, however. The evolution took place over 250 years.

During this period, there was no outside influence to the Californios' horsemanship except what came from the Iberian Peninsula. Meanwhile, there was a great renaissance going on in Europe, with a major part being the horsemanship schools in Italy, France and Spain in the development of the classical style of riding.

The California bridle horse is not a classically-trained horse. He is what could be referred to as a traditionally-trained horse. The job of cattle work dictated the movements that had to be developed. History tells us that the Spanish and Portuguese people were very proud of their horses. The horses were a major part of the culture and were very well trained. The classical riding influence that was reserved for society's elite and some within the military trickled down to the tenders of livestock, the vaqueros of the Iberian Peninsula and the newly-conquered world of North and South America.

It was not the movements performed by these classical horses that was sought, but the attitude and knowledge needed for the horses to move well. That, in turn, required the progressive development of suppleness, gymnastication and balance of the horse's body, which led to control of his mind and obedience to a rider's signals without resistance.

Some of the equipment and tools that have come to us through this discipline include the single pillar, also known as the circus pole, and long lines. The exercises so crucial to the development of a highly-educated bridle horse included work on a circle with arc or bend to the horse's body to match that of the circle being ridden. These horses of old were also schooled in straight, lateral and oblique lines with their bodies at different angles to the line of travel. Such simple maneuvers, practiced over time, raised the vaquero horse's mind and body to a high degree of performance. These are all things the cattle working bridle horse needs, regardless of the age he lives in.

The earlier conquering Moors also influenced the Iberian Peninsula with the bent leg style of riding and some of the bridle bit mouthpieces that we still use today. What came to the New World in the form of a hackamore-type device was merely a strap placed over the horse's nose with reins attached, much like what you see today in the training of the Doma Vaquera horse in Spain and Portugal. What evolved in Mexico and California over the years into our hackamore is unique in the world, and is a very technical discipline within itself.

Vaquero, in spanish, means tender of livestock. In California, Oregon, Nevada and parts of Idaho, vaquero loosely translates as buckaroo or cowboy. However, it's much more than what most people think of as a cowboy today. I was raised in the vaquero tradition in southern and central California. I have ridden bridle horses for as long as I can remember.

I started to learn how to develop or "build" them at age 15 when I started buckarooing for a living.

As of this writing, I'm 70 years old, and this journey of learning how to build a better-balanced horse will never end. It is important for both you and your horse that you enjoy the journey.

My 55 years of working cattle, the miles ridden and the long hours in the saddle, alone or with other buckaroos, was the high school and college time I spent to learn this discipline. The last sixteen years of teaching clinics in the United State and in Europe, of imparting this vaquero style, has helped me to think through and analyze precisely how I do things in the training of this style of horse. I think that has made me a better horseman.

The things I was taught and the things I have learned is what I know today. My style of riding and the steps I use to build this California-style bridle horse are a reflection of all of that. What I do is not the only way it can be done, nor the only way it is done today. But I believe this older, more methodical way builds a better horse that has the strength through his back to still be doing his job of working cattle into his old age with quality of movement.

Most of the suppling and gymnastic exercises I use to develop my horses I learned as a boy and a young man. Most of the time, the old-timers used slang western words to describe them. Up until the time I was exposed to some people in the eastern United States and Europe, I, too, used western slang, which made it difficult for the people I was trying to help to understand what I was saying. I found that beyond the world of the buckaroo there is a universal language of words, phrases and expressions to describe the movements of horses. Some of my friends have taken the time to help me learn this language. It has certainly helped me in teaching, but I have not yet mastered it in my ongoing education.

My grandfather used to say, "Patience is a virtue and you should exercise it whenever you are around livestock." Let the journey begin.

~ Mike Bridges
Halfway, Oregon
March 2010

INTRODUCTION

The vaquero-style bridle horse is one that is ridden in one hand for all work, and controlled without fingers through the reins. His primary job is to handle cattle, which includes herding, driving, cutting and sorting in a gate. In the roping of cattle, he serves as the engine to pull or as the anchor to hold. At all times, he should be a pleasure to ride.

A bridle horse is very light in the face and throughout the body, being obedient to the slightest of signals from the rider. It takes five to eight years to build what vaqueros call a "straight up bridle horse." This time is necessary to build the strength throughout the horse's back and the rest of his body so he is able to work in a collected frame for long periods of time. His body needs to be very supple with a very high degree of balance and the ability to re-balance within the stride.

Bridle horses come in all shapes, colors and breeds. It is the training that makes the bridle horse, not the pedigree or type. When you see one, it is like watching poetry in motion in its movements, with lightning response to the rider's demands.

SPECIAL NOTES

These are the guiding principles to remember when "building" a California-Style Bridle Horse.

First, last and always, you have to have FORWARD in the horse. Forward is a learned behavior. Your goal in building a California-style vaquero bridle horse is to be able to regulate and control the energy in the horse's body in all gaits and at all speeds so that all the energy comes from his hindquarters and moves forward, and he is able to go from a pure thrusting hind leg without frame (with no openness in the back) to a slower, more collected carrying hind leg with frame, and everything in between with a thrusting/carrying hind leg. This energetic forwardness is the result of DRIVE. Drive refers to the TRACTION produced on the ground from the stroke of the hind legs. In time, drive must be developed so it is powerful and explosive. This is also a learned behavior for the horse. The goal is to develop this drive as a learned behavior because it is already in him as an instinctive behavior when, in his natural environment, he takes flight from danger. When developed, good *forward* will lead to more quickness and acceleration in movement.

Second, you must have SUPPLENESS. You must be able to move all of the horse's structures anywhere you want. In time, you need suppleness developed so that he moves without bracing against your signals to him, both on the ground and in the saddle. This will give you the chance to develop LIGHTNESS TO SIGNALS.

Third, LIGHTNESS TO SIGNALS is based on three things: 1) Clarity and correctness of the signals; 2) The presentation and power of the signals; and 3) The intensity and duration of the signals. All of these factors will determine the LEVEL OF RESPONSE of the horse and help to develop INSTANT RESPONSE to signals.

Fourth, through gymnastic work, you will build a "topline" in the horse so that he has strength to sustain movements for a longer period of time. This will allow you to achieve better BALANCE AND SUSTAINING BALANCE.

Fifth, with increased BALANCE AND SUPPLENESS, you have the chance for SPEED in your work, and LIGHTNESS IN MOVEMENT without bracing.

Sixth, LIGHTNESS TO SIGNALS is not the same as LIGHTNESS IN MOVEMENT.

First you will get LIGHTNESS TO SIGNALS. Then, if the work continues to be good, you will achieve LIGHTNESS IN MOVEMENT.

Remember, without FORWARD, you can achieve none of these things.

~ MIKE

Chapter 1

EARLY TRAINING

When I get a new horse, from the very beginning my thoughts are that I'm going to build a bridle horse.

If it's a colt, I have a fresh, clean mind to work with and a body that will need a lot of development. If I'm going to re-train a horse that has past negative human experiences, I might have a horse with a troubled mind but a body with more strength. In either case, I start the process from the beginning.

So let's begin as if we're going through each step with a young horse. If I'm working with an older horse that is being re-trained, the same steps would apply but not necessarily in the same sequence.

HOW HORSES THINK

A horse does not think like a human. Horses operate entirely by memory. They live in the present, don't think about the future, but are very perceptive to what is about to happen based on their previous experiences. If there is no memory or no negative memory, the horse tends to perceive something as dangerous until it is shown to be otherwise.

In his natural environment, the horse within a herd is moved around by more dominant horses through social interaction. He understands this. His social system is designed this way. So when we begin to ask him to move his body around, with energy rather than brute force, there can be a similar acceptance and understanding between us if we do it correctly.

If the horse was raised in a box stall rather than with a herd, this fundamental social response would still be the same. It is within the horse's gene pool. For all the millions of generations of domestication of the horse, humans have not altered the flight for survival response nor the herd instinct.

What is a Colt?

When I talk about colts, I mean a horse that is a young, uneducated or slightly educated animal. His age can be just slightly under two years or six-to-eight years of age.

When we refer to a colt, we refer to a horse that has no training, very little training or is in the early stages of training. But in this day and age, you don't see many six-year-old colts anymore. Back in the 1950s, most horses weren't started until they were six years old or older. They had to be strong enough to stand the riding to do a day's work.

In educating the younger horses, the two and three year old horses, it is much easier to influence them mentally because they are still searching for their social position within the herd. They don't know where they fit. It's much easier to get them to yield mentally, i.e., to "step down."

A six-year-old horse is much firmer in his position in the herd. He knows where he stands and is much more reluctant to give up his position. So when we talk about colts, we're talking about stage of development in training, not about his sex or his age.

Later on in the schooling of this horse, I will ask him for a lot of mental concentration through physical exercises. "The mind has to be right for the body to be right and invariably you are going to have to work through the body to get the mind right," says my friend Frank Barnett.

It is a time-consuming process to build the horse physically and mentally if I expect him to reach high levels of performance. In other words, the development of the horse is <u>not</u> a casual deal.

THE ROUND PEN

I like to start in a round pen that is 60 feet in diameter. This size gives enough room so the horse does not feel trapped at the start of the groundwork and, later on in the riding work, allows enough space for the horse to be able to lope at the wall with some balance.

> **The Difference between the Lope and the Canter**
>
> The lope is a three-beat gait with a moment of suspension but with no frame on the horse. In other words, no "openness" in the back. The horse is not in a collected frame.
>
> The canter is also a three-beat gait with a moment of suspension but the body of the horse is compressed so that the spinous processes in the back are open and the thrust of the gait has lifting energy in it, along with forward energy.

Round pens 40-to-45 feet in diameter cause most horses to struggle for balance with a rider on their backs at the lope when you first start. If you force the lope at these smaller diameters, you could unintentionally build a brace in the horse's body as he struggles for balance. For me, I always prefer to not create a problem that I will have to deal with later on in the training process. A round pen can be built out of any type of material as long as it is strong enough to support the weight of a horse leaning against it or withstand the impact of a kick.

I prefer round pen walls to be straight up and down, at least six feet high, and solid at least four feet up from the ground so that neither the horse's feet, my foot nor the saddle stirrup can get hung up in the fence. Round pens with sloped walls can be good when riding because they keep your horse away from the walls. But if the horse crowds the wall and his feet hit on the slope, it can cause him to fall.

At the start of this early training, the horse does not know what is going on and can have moments of fear or panic. This is the reason I prefer the straight solid walls. This is probably the colt's first introduction to working in an arc and with slight bend in his body.

BALANCE IN ARC

In nature, the horse's preferred way to balance is on his diagonal pair of legs and feet. In other words, his front left leg moves in synchronized motion with the diagonal right hind leg. The reason for this is that nature tells the horse to stay prepared to flee in case of danger. Doing so requires that his back be in what is called a "closed" position so that he can create pure thrust with his legs.

Horses use what we call "arc balance"—balancing with a slight lateral bend throughout the length of his body—only when they play with other horses. But they don't sustain arc balance for more than a few strides.

To achieve balance with arc in his body, the horse's back must have some openness, or roundness, along the spine from the withers through the mid-back. Learning to sustain openness in the back is a learned behavior for the horse. It requires trust in the rider by the horse to allow its body to be manipulated so that he can do different movements with balance. In time, I will need a lot of control over this so that I can open the horse's back at will and he will sustain it. The shape of the round pen forms an arc. This helps hold the colt's hip in, preventing the horse from reverting to diagonal balance when I have put confinement to his body with a hand position when riding or a fixed-hand position with side reins during some of the groundwork.

Right from the start, I want the colt to understand that I can control the life in his body. So I'll drive the colt around the pen without any equipment on his body, sending energy towards his hip to drive him forward.

> **What is a "Closed" Back?**
>
> A "closed" back on a horse refers to the position of the spinous processes, which are attached to the vertebrae of the spinal column.
>
> When we refer to the back being in a "closed" position the spinous processes of the thoracic vertebrae are close together and the major muscle groups of the back, primarily the loin and lumbar muscles, are in an extended position with resistance in them.
>
> This is the position the back would need to be in to create pure thrust in the legs to go to flight or run around the racetrack flat out.
>
> When I refer to the back being "open" or a "round back," this is when the back extends itself by separating the spinous processes slightly more in the direction of an arc line and the major muscle groups in the back have extended without resistance but hold tone.
>
> In this configuration, the thrust of the legs has lifting energy along with thrusting energy, and is the position necessary to create collection or a degree of collection.

Energy, in the form of a swinging rope or me merely walking in his direction, can be directed at his mid-body to hold him to the fence. Energy directed at or ahead of his eye will cause him to change direction. Energy can be decreased by stepping back when the colt looks at me or when I want to signal him to come in.

DEVELOPING UNDERSTANDING

When I let the horse come in to me, I'll let him stay a while and touch his body on both sides. I use a soft stroking with my fingers or little pats with my hands, sometimes scratching with my fingertips. I will do whatever I think of to help calm and reassure the horse that things are going to be okay. My voice can also help if I keep the tone of my words even and the volume of my voice soft.

I will feel how much tension there is in his muscles. I will gauge whether he's tight or relaxed. Then I will send him out again and repeat this until the horse decides he wants to stay around me.

Soon the horse understands that if he leaves it is going to cost him more energy when he is out at the wall being driven around by me at the trot or lope. So he is mentally prepared to hang around as I introduce something new. Next, I'll place a ring snaffle bit in his mouth so he can begin to learn how to pick it up and support it with his tongue and hard palate.

With the horse standing near me, he should keep facing me or following me regardless of the direction I move. This is the first mental yield to me by the horse. Not much is happening yet to help the body, a little bending maybe, but I am beginning to capture the mind.

MENTAL YIELDING

When this mental yield is established, I'll halter the horse and begin to move his hindquarters and forequarters around. My horse has to learn that I can move the structures in his body at will while he's under my confinement. I'll leave the snaffle in his mouth to build more confidence in supporting the bit.

HINDQUARTERS

To move the hindquarters, I stand off from his shoulder about a foot or two and tip his head slightly toward me. Then I look at the hip of the horse and direct some energy toward it using my eyes, my hand or by swinging the end of my lead rope in the direction of his stifle joint and hind leg until the leg nearest me moves under the horse's body and slightly forward. This is an engaged forward step, something I want to develop in the horse from the first session.

Engagement is when the hind foot steps under the mass of the body and forward. Disengagement is when the foot steps across the plane of the body rather than forward. Untracking means moving from a static position to some form of motion; forward, backward, left, right, up or down.

If the horse's hind foot steps next to or behind the other hind leg, the horse is bracing, or tensing, his ribcage on the side nearest me. This is incorrect. If that's the case, I'll send more energy toward his hip until he gets it right with a forward step.

When asking the horse to disengage his hip to the right, there is no forward movement. In this step, the left hind leg moves sideways across the plane of the body.

The flexing of the ribs, or the horse bending his mid-body, is very important for the kind of work I'm going to ask the horse to do in his career as a cow horse. So right from the start I am going to do some work that will require him to bend this part of his body. If he braces, that is resistance in the muscle groups called the obliques and abdominal muscles.

When asking the horse to engage his right hind leg, the leg moves forward and across the plane of the body. On the stroke of that leg, the horse moves forward.

When the horse braces, the hind leg that I'm trying to move forward and under his body will instead move sideways across the plane of the body. This is disengagement, not engagement.

Bracing—the resistance in muscles in the horse when we ask the horse to move different body parts—is to be expected and can show itself in two ways.

Testing Your Program

A brace or resistance in one or more body parts happens because the horse wants to do things his way, not your way. This is more of a social brace. In other words, he is testing your program, questioning your authority. He would like to be one rung higher than you on the herd's social ladder.

The other form of bracing comes about as we teach new movements to our horse and he does not yet have the physical ability to carry balance through the movement because not all the structures in his body are in good alignment. Therefore, he braces a part or parts of his body to try to help himself balance.

All braces need to be addressed as soon as they show up by increasing the energy in the signals, either with more motion, pressure or both. Left unanswered, braces in the horse's body will come back to haunt you later when you put speed to your work.

Forequarters

After I get his hips working well in both directions, I will start on the forequarters. To begin with, forequarters are usually more difficult to move than hindquarters. (Standing in an unframed position, a horse has something between 60-to-65 percent of his weight on his forequarters, he is built heavy to the front end.)

Standing with my body parallel to the horse between his eye and shoulder, I will send energy toward his eye and neck area to ask the horse to move his forequarters away from me in a circle. I want the forequarters to move faster than the hips are moving and, in time, I expect the inside hind foot (on the inside of the bend) to become a pivot point as the forequarters move around in a circle away from the pressure of my signals.

Teaching the horse to turn around to the right from the ground, before riding him. I'm looking for the left front foot to reach forward and across the plane of the body ahead of the other front foot. The horse's inside right hind leg to be the main pillar of support.

I will look for his front leg on my side to step across but ahead of his other front leg as he moves in a circle. If the front leg nearest me steps next to or behind the other front leg, it indicates he's not flexing his ribcage on the opposite side as he should. If this happens, I will increase the energy I direct toward him until I get the correct movement. If I have to, I will physically push the colt around to help him find it. Once I get a few correct steps, I will quit touching him and go back to using motion from my body to create energy to drive the colt.

As the horse moves, I'll need to move with him while holding my position between his eye and his shoulder. When I stop moving, he should stop, too. This represents the first time for my colt to learn the mechanics of the turn-around.

Moving the Jaws and Atlas

I am pulling the horse's face toward me while at the same time pushing the lower jaw away from me, using a slight torquing action. I want the horse to release at the atlas-axis joint. This can help him to be relaxed in the poll and mandible of the jaw. Any tension in the poll or jaw of the horse will show up also in the back of the horse as tension.

The jaw as well as the atlanto-occipital joint and the atlas-axis joint of the horse need to stay relaxed throughout the training process. Any tension in the jaw or poll will create a corresponding tension or brace in his back and can hinder saliva flow in his mouth; consequently, the term "the dry-mouthed horse."

Standing at the side of the horse near his head, I'll place one hand over the bridge of his nose and my other hand on the large jaw muscle on the side of his face. Using a slight torquing action, I will try to move the jaw under the throatlatch area just a slight amount, the same as if he were laterally flexed in that direction. If the horse braces against my hands, I will hold this slight pressure until he releases his atlas-axis joint where his head is attached to the spine. Then I'll rub his face over the eye with soft strokes to let him know he did well.

This is just another step in manipulating the horse's physical structures from the ground. My goal is to teach the horse that he can move his jaw and poll away from pressure by himself and that when he does, he can be relaxed.

Shaking the horse back with the lead rope is part of the process of teaching the horse to stand in his own space.

WORK ETHIC AND PATIENCE

I believe it is very important that my horse learn both a good work ethic and patience. In their natural environment, horses never work. They would much rather eat 17 hours a day, drink some water, have some social activity with other members of the herd and sleep short periods of time. The horse is the master of the catnap.

So at this point in the training, I like to teach my horse to stand still. I like to say, "My horse can stand in his own space." It is a great little thing to teach him patience and to be obedient, and can be helpful when you shoe him or have him on the end of a rope while doctoring cattle.

With a lead rope on my colt—I like a rope 12-to-14 feet in length that has some weight to it so that it can create good energy—I will get out in front of him and ask him to keep his body straight. I like to be three-to-six feet away from him. Next, I will shake the lead rope in a side-to-side motion, starting softly and increasing the intensity of the motion until he takes a step back. The instant he steps back, I stop the rope from moving. Then I ask for another step backward.

After a few steps, I'll stand still. I want him to stand still and keep his eye on me. If he makes a move forward, I'll correct him by shaking the rope until he backs up, starting with a soft shake and building the energy until I get the step or steps backward I want. If he takes two steps forward, I will move him backward three. If he gets nervous and has to move, I will let him go backward but not forward.

Some horses can be a little tough to get this started in an open area like the round pen. Not knowing what to do or what you want from them, they will try to run around you. To deal with this type of behavior, I will go to an alleyway where it's easier to block both sides. This helps the horse. In a short time, he will understand what I am after. In a few sessions, he will stand still for quite a while. Soon, I can back him up a long way with a mere shake of a rope.

When I do this in a grassy area, I don't let the horse eat. I ask him to keep his head up. Horses will learn to use dropping the head as a form of evasion. Obviously, this takes their mental focus off you. No matter where I am, if I park my horse and ask him to stay, I don't let him put his nose to the ground.

Teaching the horse to step-by next to a barrier with energy on both sides of his body. Once he learns to accept this you can send him anyplace: into a single horse trailer, across a rock slide or put him in a closet. I'm also asking him to do this from a change in elevation, step-up and step-down, to add an element of rebalance to the exercise.

Working the filly from my horse puts me in a little safer place, especially if the colt or mature horse is disrespectful of my space, or what I am asking for. Here I'm asking this filly to move her hip to the left.

Teaching this filly to drive forward from the hip. Everything needs to happen from the hip forward.

Moving the front end around the back end. This filly is mad. She was mad about everything to start with, but she got past it by doing the work asked of her.

A little tow-truck work. I would like this filly to follow a feel.

Driving the filly around in a circle. She is now starting to relax and listen to the signals.

The end of the work. This filly has made a change mentally. She now knows she will be asked to do things and will have to comply. Toward the last part of the work there were movements when the filly relaxed, but you can see in this picture the resistance in the body. I could feel it with my hand, she is not done testing the program. This testing and resistance will dissipate in time as she learns how to balance and rebalance in the different movements she needs to learn to do her job. Through all this you need to be careful not to suppress the horse's personality. Emphasize it, let it develop, and you will end up with a better horse.

Lass Rope Work

Lass comes from the word lasso. The rope can also be called a reata when it is braided out of rawhide. This is the rope vaqueros or buckaroos use to catch cattle or horses and other things that walk on this earth. I realize that not everybody uses this type of long rope, but it's always been a big part of my style of doing my job, so let's discuss it.

Horses can have a hard time dealing with objects coming towards them like tumbleweeds, paper, rabbits, ropes and even cattle. As a prey animal, the horse is very sensitive to motion. Instinct tells him that all things moving toward him are dangerous until proven otherwise.

The horse's eye is designed to detect motion, not sharpness of image like the human eye. The horse has an oblong pupil in his eye and can gather more light than we can. He also has a reflector in his eye that gives him the ability to use light twice, which allows him to detect motion much faster than a human. He does not need to see the stripes on the tiger; he needs to see the tiger preparing to move.

Everything that moves or has motion on this earth creates energy. The horse is very aware of everything around it that is creating energy. It is his first line of defense along with his other senses that tell him when he needs to flee. Once a horse overcomes the fear of a moving object, learning that it is not dangerous, things get better. By roping the different parts of his body, he can be helped to understand that not all motion coming toward him is a threat to his survival.

Roping different body parts of the horse can really help him get used to big energy coming toward the body. Also, when the rope is pulled tight to yield to pressure.

Starting to move the front end to the right and left.

Driving the colt to the right with the rope over the shoulders and around the hip.

Around the barrel of the colt.

Things are OK.

Without the halter and lead rope on the horse, I will start out with him standing near me. I will use the coils of the rope to rub him all over his body. If he can't handle the rope touching him and he leaves, that's okay. I'll just drive him off to the wall of the round pen. When he asks to come back in, I start over.

As this gets better, I'll place a large loop over his hips and apply a little pressure there. If he stays, this is good. If he leaves, that's okay, too. I just bring him back and start again. I'll do this with all his body parts including his legs and finish with the rope around the barrel of the horse

After he gets to the point where none of this is a big deal in the first sessions, I will send him to the wall with forward motion in his body. While I stand in the center of the pen, I will rope the different body parts, always being careful not to hit the face or eye of the horse with the rope. I want him to get to a point where he will stand still when roped and come to me when I apply pressure to the rope when it is around one of his body parts.

How many sessions it takes for him to become unafraid depends on the personality of the horse. This is not a fix-all for things that might bother a horse, but it can be very helpful.

The purpose of all of this groundwork is to develop trust, understanding and respect between the horse and me. I want him to learn that I can and will control the life in his body, and that I can move his different body parts.

The First Saddling

When the time comes for the saddle to go on for the first time, my first choice is to have my colt standing with me in the center of the round pen without a halter on. If all this work is done with a halter on the colt, and only a little or none of it is completed without it, the colt learns the difference. The level of respect from the colt will not be as high when there is physical restraint. This should be remembered for all of our work. If my colt has shown a claustrophobic attitude, I'll halter him to help him hang around.

Up to this point, I have touched him on his body with my hands and the coils of my lass rope, progressively desensitizing him to an unusual and potentially scary feel. Next, I will start with the saddle blanket. I will rub it over his body, put it in place on his back and slap it a few times. I do this from both sides of the colt.

Horses have very little crossover learning ability compared to a human. Consequently, I want to expose both sides of the horse to everything. One side may be more sensitive or have more resistance than the other. I need to recognize this and adjust my training accordingly so both sides at some point end up equal and balanced.

Standing at his shoulder, I will swing the saddle up and place it on his back in one smooth motion (I want my cinch held by the keeper on my saddle so it does not hit his leg when I swing my saddle onto his back). I don't want to throw it at him or slap it down on his back. After it's on, I'll tuck the blankets up into the gullet of the saddle. Then I'll let the cinch down. When I'm ready to cinch up, I'll stand by his shoulder again and reach under for the cinch using my left hand or a hook, keeping my eye on the hind legs.

As I pull the cinch up, I'll use my left hand against his left shoulder to help brace him as I tighten the latigo. I want it tight enough so the saddle won't slip under his belly if he makes a hard move but not so tight that he can't expand his ribcage as he moves.

At this point I like to leave the pen and let the horse move off and find his own way. Most horses won't blow up if your other work has been done with quality, and trust and respect has started to develop.

When I think he has had enough time moving on his own, I'll enter the round pen and begin to drive him forward at the walk, trot and lope and do some more lass rope work. When I begin to rope my saddle, the sound of the rope hitting the leather will be a new experience for him.

Forward to the Backup

Now that I have my horse saddled and moving around without feeling bothered, I like to do some more work from the ground to control the life in his body going forward and backward. This gives the horse a chance to feel the change of movement within his body structures, the expansion and contraction of his mid-body with the saddle on his back, and the cinch around his ribcage.

This can be a big deal to some colts. Confinement to the horse's body, like cinches or other things that restrict movement, can bring out the claustrophobia in a horse.

With a halter and lead rope on my colt, I will stand at his shoulder. Using a light stick or whip, I'll ask him to move forward by tapping his hip at the lumbar-sacral joint or behind the stifle joint. As he moves forward, I'll keep the energy directed at his hip.

When I want him to stop and start backward, I will move the stick ahead of his eye and create some motion with the stick until he starts to move backward. If he can't find the stop and doesn't back up from the motion of my stick, I'll tap him lightly on the bridge of the nose until he starts back. When he does, I'll go back to simply motioning with the stick. I want to get this developed to where the colt follows the motion of my body forward and backward.

At first, I won't be very critical that he match the same steps going back as going forward. I might ask him for five steps forward and only three back, or three forward and five back. I'll practice a sequence two or three times and then move him forward about 10 feet or more before repeating the sequence again. When my colt understands what I'm after, then I'll go to a set sequence such as five steps forward and five steps backward, repeating it three-to-five times. I also like to use three-step sequences at the start. This is a little less demanding mentally and physically for the young horse.

Think Time

After I've completed three-to-five sequences, I move the horse forward to let him relax. This gives him time to come down physically. But more importantly, it allows him to think about what has just transpired.

I don't precisely know how think time works in the horse. But I know that it does work. If you train on a movement in the morning and give the horse a break and work on the same thing again later in the day, the horse will usually be better. If you turn a horse out for two weeks or two months, when

Forward to the back-up. This exercise has a lot of value for a number of different things...

...it teaches the horse that you can influence his hip to drive forward, to engage his hip when he stops...

...or to keep his hip slightly engaged while picking up his front feet as he backs up.

you bring him back in to go back to work, he will be as good as or better than when you turned him out if your training has been correct. These short periods of relax time between sets of sequences seem to help also.

As your horse gets good at this, you will see him driving more from the hips and putting more weight over his hock joints. This also helps him learn to transfer some of his front end weight to the area behind his 14th thoracic vertebra in the middle of his back.

> ### The 14th Thoracic Vertebra
>
> On almost all horses, the 14th thoracic vertebra is located approximately two inches behind the end of the withers, regardless of how the withers are shaped. It is the strongest part of the horse's back to support weight.
>
>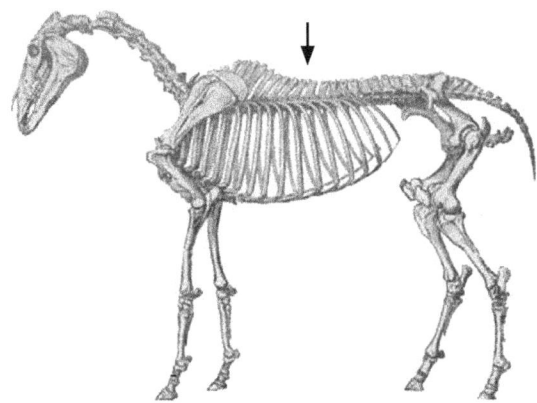
>
> When in motion, the 14th thoracic vertebra is the area of the horse's back where he balances and re-balances himself. It is not his center of gravity.
>
> The closer the rider can sit over the 14th thoracic vertebra, the easier it is to have positive influence to both ends of the horse.
>
> The 14th thoracic vertebra is the dividing line in his body to read signals. Any pressure applied to the horse ahead of the 14th will affect the forward ribs, shoulders, neck and/or head of the horse. Pressure applied behind the 14th will immediately affect the hips.
>
> Because this part of the horse's anatomy is so important in the understanding of an application of signals, and because I need to refer to it so often, I'll simply call it the "14th."

LIGHT FIXED-HAND WORK

Before I start to ride my horse in the hackamore or snaffle bit, I want him to understand how to yield his face in a manner that will stretch the nuchal ligament in the neck to create some opening of the withers. Some light fixed-hand work can help him learn to flex his head, neck and mid-body while moving forward.

With my horse wearing a snaffle, I take two of my piggin' strings—a short, light rope seven-to-eight feet in length used for tying cattle—and attach one end to the snaffle ring and run it to my cinch ring, or through my stirrup and back up to the back saddle rigging. The other string goes from the snaffle ring on the other side of the horse and to a position on my saddle slightly higher than the first one. The string that has the lowest point of pull will be the direction of travel.

I set my string on the side of the colt that indicates direction so that it brings his head just off the centerline of his body, with his nose ahead of the vertical. This will cause him to look in the direction of travel. The string on the other side of his body is set as a supporting rein just as if I was riding him. By doing this, I want to create a slight lateral arc in his body.

A word of caution: Do not leave a horse standing in fixed hands. I do not want my horse standing still any longer than necessary when I have put a fixed-rein position on him. I need to get motion in his body going forward or backward. As soon as I have the horse rigged up, I put forward motion into his body. If I don't, he will learn to lean on the bit.

Next, I'll drive him forward around the pen at all three gaits: walk, trot and canter. I look for the inside string to become soft and for the horse to hold that softness for more strides. By setting him in fixed-hands, I am asking him to hold an arc balance throughout his body. I observe the structures in his body; how his feet fall, whether he is bracing with the inside ribcage, whether his outside hip is in alignment with the rest of his body.

As my horse becomes soft and holds the softness for more and more strides, I will see the other parts of his body set themselves in better alignment with less tension. After I have obtained some progress on one side, I'll change my strings to work my horse going in the other direction.

BIOMECHANICS OF FIXED-HANDS

The energy coming through the horse's body from his hips forward causes contraction to the abdominal and oblique muscles. This, in turn, causes the base of the neck to raise up into the shoulders, which changes the shape of the neck and brings the face more towards the vertical, allowing the horse to get soft to the fixed-hands rein position.

As he finds this softness and position of balance and creates a memory of it, he will seek it quicker and quicker. At this stage of training, I'm asking for only slight bend off of the centerline of his body and only enough face toward the vertical to maintain good contact so he can't push his head and neck back to the counter side.

> **What is Fixed-Hands?**
>
> When referring to "fixed hands," I mean the use of side reins that are attached to the saddle or to a surcingle in different positions to create various influences to the face of the horse and to create influence to the nuchal ligament in the neck.
>
> When riding a horse and using hands to influence the reins to create a position to get the horse to do something, your hands should stay in a fixed position until you are done with that movement in order to help the horse understand and maintain a frame.
>
> However, if the horse has a resistance from lack of understanding or lack of balance, he could move your hands because no one has the strength the horse has in his neck or body.
>
> When we create a fixed position with a side rein, he cannot move that fixed-hand position even when there is a resistance in the horse from lack of understanding or balance.

Some light fixed-hand work can help the horse learn to flex his head, neck and mid-body while moving forward. The lateral flexion of the face stretches the nuchal ligament in the horse's neck, which opens the spinous processes at the withers. Driving the hips forward creates contraction of the abdominal and oblique muscles, which allows the mid-back to open.

I'm not after a lot of flexion in the beginning. The amount of lateral flexion and vertical flexion needs to be just enough to prevent him from being able to push back to the counter side. If he pushes back, he's trying to get back to diagonal balance (opposite hip to opposite shoulder) instead of maintaining the balance line through the arc of his body along the spinal column. It will take a few years for the horse to be able to achieve maximum bend in the body and openness in his back while being able to maintain it for long periods. The strength in the top line of the horse, the back and neck, needs to be developed over time.

Use of the Single Pillar or Circus Pole

The single pillar, also known as the circus pole, is not new. There are depictions of a single pillar being used in the French school in the 1500s and in Greco-Roman art long before that. I learned about it a long time ago from my friend Gary Baumer, who learned it from a circus trainer; hence the name circus pole.

The primary purpose of the single pillar is to teach a horse balance in arc. There are other uses also, such as teaching rollback work and sidepass work, as well as transitions of gait up and down.

If you lunge your horse using a line from you to the horse, you'll find that every time he goes out of arc balance he moves your hand. If he really goes out of balance, he can move your whole body off of the spot where you're standing. But when the rope or line from the horse goes around the pole and then to your hand, when he goes out of balance he bumps the pole, which does not move.

This requires the horse to immediately re-align his body to get back into balance or use more energy to continue forward out of balance.

Without a doubt, horses understand the expenditure of energy. By their nature, they will always take the way that uses the least amount of energy if they can find it. When your horse works in the round pen in fixed-hands, or you have him on a lunge line, and he goes out of balance because of a brace or misalignment of a structure, he can go quite a few strides before it starts to cost him more energy to maintain his forward movement. When you have the circus pole as the pillar that the lunge rope goes around, the instant he goes out of balance, he pays for it by using more energy than if he were to remain in arc balance.

Consequently, he will begin to seek the adjustment for re-balancing in arc, and learn how to carry himself in arc balance for more and more strides.

Placement of the Pole

Setting a pole in the ground is a pretty cheap investment. I used to move my circus pole from cow camp to cow camp, and I used it in the development of my horses through all their years of training. There have been lots of times I didn't have access to a round pen, but I was always able to have a pole in the ground to help teach balance to a higher degree while going forward on a circle, and the re-balancing that goes on between the transitions of gaits up and down.

Top of a circus pole and one of the ways to fix the rope. This would create good drag on the rope if the horse was attached to the rope going through the eye-bolt and his body was moving to the left.

It is much easier for my horse to learn these things without me on his back. He has only to balance and re-balance himself as he learns. He does not have to adjust for my weight and the little mistakes I might make controlling my weight in motion.

The placement of a circus pole is important. Putting it close to fences or buildings or other structures can create an adverse influence to the body of the horse. The less outside energy, the better. Outside energy has a tendency to help shape the body of the horse.

As much as possible, I want the horse to seek the alignment of the structures in his body for balance without outside influence. So I like to have 30 feet of open area from the pole in all directions. If I can't get that much space around the pole I will still use it recognizing that balance is going to develop more slowly, especially at the start when the horse is farther from the pole. When the horse can do canter work closer to the pole, the effect of the outside influences diminish.

Using the pole as a fulcrum to help this colt learn to change direction from a signal. The first move of that change is that he moves his shoulder away from me.

> **Different Kinds of Circus Poles**
>
> A circus pole can be made out of different kinds of materials; wood or steel, for instance. It can be different heights or can be constructed so it can telescope to different heights.
>
> The circus pole will have the most advantage for its purpose if it's in an open area without obstructions like walls, barns, fences or corrals around it. Obstructions cause an influence to the horse as he tries to conform his body to the arc you're trying to work him on.
>
> The circus pole can be made with a top that swivels. This makes the management of the rope between the horse and your hands easier than if that rope is just wrapped around the body of the pole. It can also have a lifting effect to the base of the horse's neck when you start to work in fixed-hand rein positions.
>
> If you use the rope around the body of the pole, then how you place it around the pole will have an affect on the position of the horse's head as he moves forward.
>
> If the rope goes from the horse's head to the inside of the pole, then around the pole and to your hand, the horse will have a tendency to look deeper into the direction he is going.
>
> If the rope goes from the horse's head around the outside of the pole and back to your hand, the horse will have a tendency to look straighter forward in the direction of his travel.

I would like the ground I'm working on to be level and not too deep, not more than three-to-five inches. The horse needs to be able to get his feet off the ground and back on the ground very quickly or he will use up too much energy too fast, and it will be too much of a struggle for him. You can't force him to find balance. You have to set it up so he can.

Patterning the Horse on the Pole

When I first start a horse on the pole, I "pattern" him without confinement to his body, meaning no snaffle bit and no saddle. I want him to experience the pole for the first time with the least amount of mental stress as possible.

With just a halter on the horse, I will fix a rope about 35 feet in length to the halter, take a wrap around the pole and drive him forward on the circle out at about 30 feet from the pole. If I want the horse to look in the direction that he is going, when I take a wrap on the pole, I will wrap to the inside of the pole. If I want the horse to be straighter with less bend to his head and neck going forward on the circle, I wrap to outside of the pole.

This means the horse is working on a 60-foot circle.

I want to work him at the walk, trot and lope. If my horse is lazy and does not want to go forward, I'll bring him in closer where I can reach him with a whip or a stick to control the life in his body. With the flight instinct so powerful within the horse, you would think that going forward would be easy. But you will find with a lot of horses that when some restraint is applied to their bodies, their forward motion can get dull.

With a lot of horses, we have to work to get them to bring their life up at the instant we ask, and to maintain it. It may or may not show up in the round pen. But if it shows up there, now is the time to address it. Don't wait until you start riding them.

I work one direction on the pole at a time. After he's going forward at about 30 feet from the pole at all gaits, I will start to bring him in closer to the pole a couple of feet at a time. At some point in bringing him closer to the pole and me, I'll find a place where he will begin to struggle to lope, which is caused by a loss of balance. I want him to lope with his shoulders perpendicular to the ground and not lean in with his inside shoulder overloaded. Overloading is caused by the outside hind leg striking the ground outside the bend of his body. What causes this? It occurs when the ribcage straightens itself ahead of the 14th thoracic vertebra.

When I find that spot on the circle, I won't ask him to lope but work him only in the trot and walk for a few rounds. Then, I'll move him closer to the pole to find where he struggles at the trot. Again, I want him to trot upright. From that point, I walk him in toward the pole going forward with good life until he is having trouble holding his balance.

At that point, I'll stop him, and repeat everything going in the new direction. I usually have to pattern a horse only once before I'm ready to bring my fixed-hand work to the pole.

There is really very little value to pole work without the fixed-hands. If you work a horse without confinement to his body, he'll naturally go back to a diagonal balance because that is what nature tells him he should do in order to keep his back closed so he can instantly flee if he feels danger.

This tracking on an arc line with bend in his body to match the arc of the line of travel is something he can certainly do, but it is a learned behavior for him to maintain it. Once the pattern work is done and my horse has a good understanding to go forward on the circle, and he will walk within six feet of the pole, I'm ready to begin my fixed-hand work.

I put my snaffle bit on the horse over his halter. I like to use a rope or string halter. I attach my lunge rope to the halter with the bottom loop of the halter inside the chinstrap of the snaffle bit. I set my fixed-hands with the same rein positions I used in the round pen.

There are so many rein positions that can be used for slight or major changes in the frame of the horse that I do not want to get into all of them now. Let's leave it with saying that fixed-hands is similar to when you are riding your horse with two hands. The changes and little nuances you do with your hands have similar effects. Think about them and you can find most of the fixed-hand positions.

Working a horse on the pole with light contact. The horse has cut in on the circle causing the middle of the rope to be almost on the ground. The horse needs to be drove out more. I should have read that quicker and directed more energy toward the mid-body of the horse.

What to Look For

After rigging my fixed-hand positions, I'll send my horse out on the circle to the same distance as before, about 30 feet, to see if he can handle the canter. Most times he is going to need to be farther out from the pole than he was with just the halter. What I'm looking for is where he can canter with some balance. When I find that spot, that's where I want to do the work of developing him to the point that he can make good transitions from trot to canter.

I look for him to prepare his body as I send more energy towards his hips to drive him forward. Does he come into the fixed hands, or, put another way, yield his face down and in and hold softness through the transition? For him to get to this point in his training, I'll need to do a lot of up-and-down transitions of gait. Making transitions is how he will find the balance and his own ability to re-balance. As this develops, I will start to ask him to make more revolutions around the pole and will start to work on speeds within gaits.

In time, I want him to be able to canter very slowly with some openness at the withers and mid-back. I also want him to be able to speed up the canter by lengthening his stride rather than taking quicker steps. That means going longer within the stride when I send more energy towards his hip.

I will also work on his walk-to-trot transitions at this distance from the pole. In each session, I want to do enough at the canter to see the horse put effort into the work, and to see when he makes a change. When he appears to be trying, I will stop the work at that distance and bring him in closer.

I don't want the horse to stop going forward during this change. I'll coil my rope until he's closer to the pole where I want to do the walk and trot work. Again, I need to find the spot where he can trot with some balance but is struggling a little.

For instance, say my horse can trot with balance at 12 feet from the pole but at 11 feet 6 inches he is having a little trouble maintaining balance. This is the place I want to develop the trot. When it gets good, at whatever distance I set it in relationship to the pole, I'm ready to work the gait closer to the pole.

I don't want to get in a hurry. I want to take the time to develop the smooth transitions up and down. I want to watch for the structures in the body to change, where the feet hit the ground in relation to the mass of the body. Are the braces first seen during his early transitions now gone? I don't want to leave that distance from the pole until the horse is really good. I must be patient. I want it to develop correctly.

Last part of the first work on the pole, asking the horse to drive forward at the walk around the pole. In time he will be able to bend his body more and get closer to the pole. You have not gotten all the value from the pole until your horse can canter this close to the pole. This could take a few years.

Reaching the Goal

At all gaits, at all distances, you have not gotten all the potential out of the pole until your horse can canter at the pole with his shoulders perpendicular to the ground. This takes a long time. Perhaps years. It is a highly developed maneuver, and you will be proud of your horse when he achieves this level of ability.

After the trot work is done, bring him in closer and walk him around the pole as close as he can get. Again, you want him to struggle a little to maintain his arc balance. Ask him to walk with good life. Drive him forward. Within this small circle, you are looking for his outside front foot to begin to step over and in front of the inside front foot. You also want to see his rear inside hind leg pivot more under the hip instead of behind it.

Changes in the Horse

A lot of times, this is where you will get the first big flexions in the ribcage. The energy from his hip forward through his body is what gets him to walk a tighter circle. The pole keeps him from falling through the middle of the circle. After good effort, stop, change the fixed-hand positions to the other side, and work in the other direction starting from where he can canter.

After a few sessions like this that begin where he can canter, then where he can trot, and finally at the pole in the walk, your horse will start to hunt for the pole. Two things happen mentally in the horse. He will remember that as he works in closer to the pole at a slower gait, he expends less energy and the pole is where you stop the session and let him quit working.

I want my colt to hunt the pole for a while so he will give me a big effort when walking around it. This helps teach him a work ethic. It's also the beginning work for teaching him both a turn and a turn-around with arc in his body that my bridle horse will need to work cattle. When the horse has developed to the point where I have to constantly hold energy directed at his mid-body to hold him off the pole, I will change the work pattern.

> ### Use of Whips and Sticks
>
> Whips and sticks are an extension of your arm to create energy. They can be used in ground schooling your horse with great effect and they can also be used when riding your horse with great effect.
>
> Every whip or stick will generate a different amount of energy with the same amount of movement. Whippy whips tend to create more forward in the horse. Dull whips or sticks create more bounce or lifting effect in the gait.
>
> Whips can have great value in helping the person create the amount of energy needed from the horse in whatever movement he's doing in the moment. What length or type of whip you would use with one horse in a particular situation might be entirely different for the next horse in the same situation.
>
> The horse's personality and level of training at that moment plays a big part in what whip or stick would be appropriate in the situation for the movement you're trying to create.

When I have finished the work at the walk close to the pole, I'll send him out again and do some more trot or canter work before I stop him and change direction. When I stop my horse, I want to give him the same signal each time. Later on in his training, when I start to change directions or start the rollback work, this will be very helpful.

SIGNALS AND POSITIONS AT THE POLE

The signal I use to stop my horse at the pole is to bring my driving whip across the front of my body and set up a block out in front of his face. When he stops, I want him to stand there. I'll then go out to him to make the rein changes, then start him in the other direction.

My body position in relation to the horse is the same as my work in the round pen but is much more critical. In the round pen I do most of my work from the center. With the circus pole, the pole is in the center and I need to move around it as my horse moves forward. This positions me at the hip of the horse. If I am too slow getting around the pole, this will cause the horse to slow down as his energy will run into my back. If I am too fast getting around the pole, too much of my energy will hit his mid-body, driving him out of the circle. It will take some time to master the body positions around the pole as you work your horse, but it is worth it.

A change in direction from right to left on the pole.

THE FIRST RIDE

My colt is now prepared mentally and physically for the first ride. If I have any doubt, I'm going to do more groundwork. It is safer for me and a better deal for the horse.

Right now, I want him to learn to stand still while I get on, whether it is from the fence or the ground. I don't just step into the stirrup and swing up onto a colt. I introduce mounting by stepping into the stirrup and going part way up where I can balance my upper body over his back so that he can balance himself. While I'm leaning over him, I'll pat the other side of his body and move the stirrup leather around. When I sense he is okay with this, then I get astride his back and into the stirrups. If he moves, I'll check him with my lass rope or the halter rope. After I'm on him, I don't ask him to move right away. I would like him to learn patience and not move until I ask him.

For the first ride on my colt, I like to use my lass rope or a halter to help guide him around the round pen. My lass rope gives me the advantage of having nothing on his head so there is no trap on his mind. If he gets scared he can leave and I can't pull on him, which will usually scare him more. He can't really go any place except around the round pen.

In using my lass rope, I put a loose loop around the base of his neck where it joins the shoulders. Holding the rope in one hand and the coils in the other, I use my coils to turn the horse by creating motion up by his eye on the opposite side from the direction I want to go. In other words, I move my coils by his right eye to cause him to turn to the left and vice versa. When I want him to go straight ahead around the pen I hold the rope coils over the saddle horn. In a short time, my coil movement left and right from the saddle horn will get a change of direction from my colt.

With the loop around the base of the neck, I wait for the colt's body to indicate that it wants to slow down or stop. Then I will apply pressure with the loop to the bottom of the neck, and ask for the stop. I must also remember to quit riding with my body. In a short time, pressure at the base of the neck will stop my horse along with my body signal.

If I use a halter and lead rope to help guide him, I usually pass it over his head, and then ask for the direction change. If he gets scared and has to leave, I try not to take hold of his face with the halter rope. With a lot of colts, this will only make them feel trapped.

Sometimes un-tracking or moving them forward can be a problem. I want them to start from the hip, and will encourage that area with energy from my legs directed back toward the hips. If I need more energy, I'll use the coils of my rope or the end of my halter rope. After I get some movement, I want the colt to go forward at all three gaits. His life has begun as our helper and we hope it ends up being more than keeping our feet out of the rocks.

Human Riding Influence

Whatever your style of riding, you have to use your whole body if you are going to be able to influence your horse to high levels of movements with balance. Whenever the horse moves, regardless of in what direction it is—forward, backward or to the right or left—it requires more than one structure in his body to be in correct alignment for him to complete the movement with balance, and can require re-balancing during the movement.

This requires the person riding the horse to be able to send signals to many areas of the horse's body at the same time.

Consequently, we need to learn to ride the horse using all parts of our body at the same time. We should ride with the mind, the upper body, the pelvis, legs and hands to get the best combinations of signals applied to the body of the horse. The more direct and enhancing signals you can give your horse, the more understanding there is between you.

We all ride a little differently and there are a lot of ways to signal the horse that can be correct. As we get into the riding exercises that I use to develop the bridle horse, I will explain the combinations of body signals I use to influence the movement, and the biomechanics of the horse to complete the movement.

Chapter 2

THE HACKAMORE AS A DISCIPLINE

The *hackamore* (in Spanish *la jáquima*, meaning headstall with the noseband), used in this vaquero style of riding, has evolved over the last 450 years. It began primarily in Mexico and what is now California. The complete hackamore consists of a bosal (rawhide), a "hanger" (or headstall), which is a single strip of latigo leather, and a **mecáte** (rope for reins, which traditionally is made out of mane hair from the horse).

Within the last 120 years, its use has spread to other states in the American West as well as throughout the world. History tells us that the principles of using a hackamore-type device to control forward motion of the horse came from the Asian and European continents. It was being used extensively on the Iberian Peninsula at the time the explorers came to the New World.

These hackamore devices were more like a strap around the nose of the horse with reins attached. A device like it is still used today in Spain and Portugal in the training of the Doma Vaquera horse.

What evolved in California and Mexico is a braided rawhide piece of equipment, oblong in shape. It has room enough so that when it is around the nose of the horse, the sides—called bars—can be away from the face but still be pliable enough so that they can be close to the side of the face. We refer to this piece of equipment as a bosal.

DESIGN OF THE BOSAL

Bosals are braided in different thicknesses. They are measured by the diameter of the bars, which range from one inch to 7/8, 3/4, 5/8, 1/2, 3/8 or 5/16 of an inch. They also vary in length from nose button to heel knot anywhere from 13 inches long down to nine inches.

The diameter of the bars determine what size the bosal is. The top of the bosal is called the nose button. This will be braided larger than the bars. Also, it may be braided round or flat. It may be the same diameter from one end to the other or have a bulge in the middle.

The nose button is the part of the bosal that sits on the nose of the horse between the eyes and the nostrils. At the end or bottom of the bars is the heel knot that holds the bars together. The bar consists of a core under an outer braid. The core can be made of rawhide (untanned animal hide), leather or rope, and can be either braided, twisted or twisted and sewn.

The outer braid around the core is braided in varying numbers of strands called plaits. The braid can be 12, 14, 16, 18 plaits or more. The fewer number of strands in the braid, the sharper the feel will be to the side of the horse's face and the more intense the signal will be from the rider. The bar of the bosal is one continuous braided piece from the heel knot through the nose button and back around to the heel knot. How the core is constructed, along with the outside braid, is what contributes to the resiliency of the entire bosal. When you squeeze the bars of the bosal with your hands, the bosal should have "life" or "spring" to it and should move back out to its original shape when you release your hand.

I would never use a bosal that had a cable or some other type of metal for the core. It doesn't have any natural life and is too heavy. All the bosals I use are light in weight. For that matter, a true bosal contains no metal at all. The piece of equipment known as a "mechanical hackamore" is more akin to what could be called a bitless bridle than to a real hackamore or bosal.

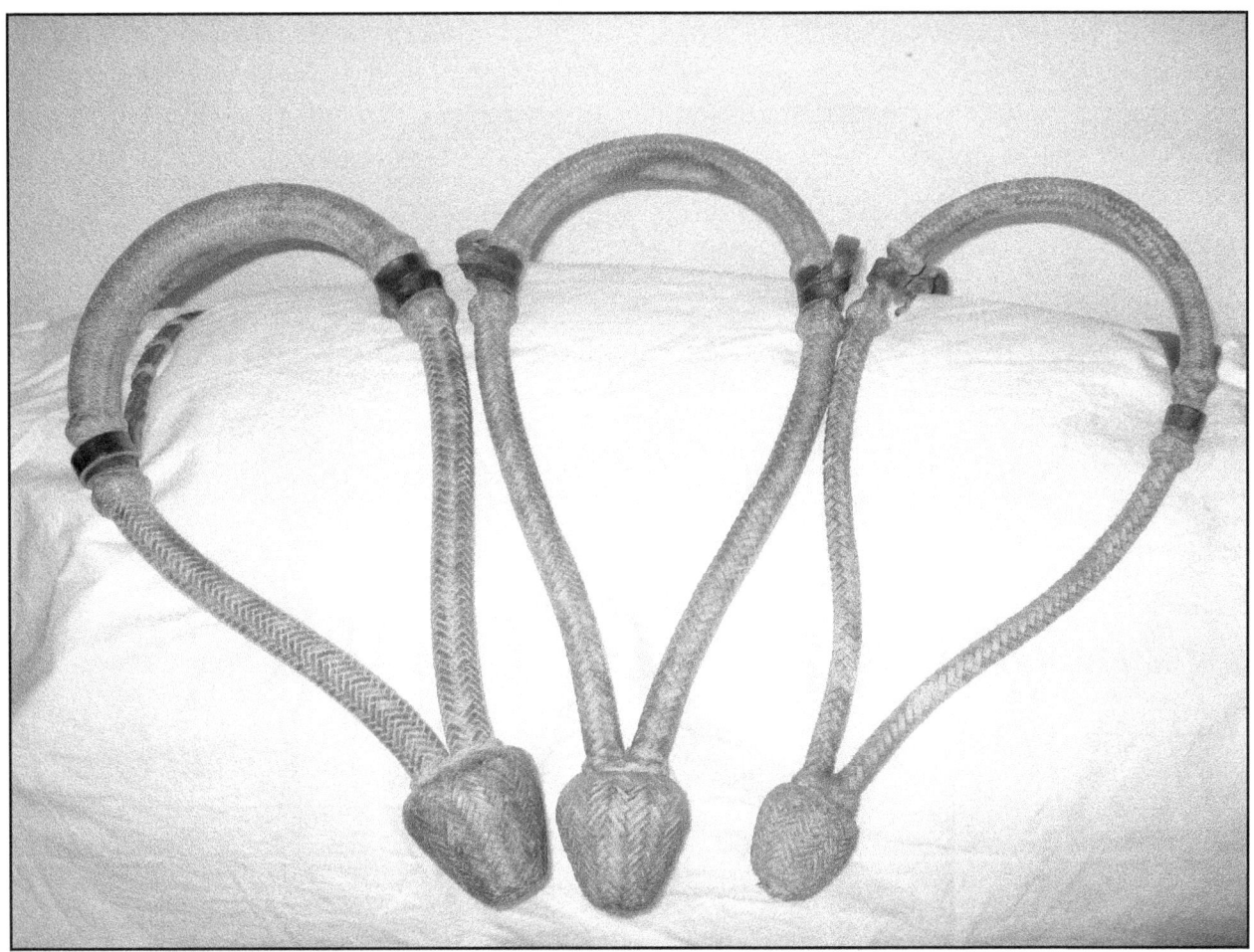

The three sizes of bosals I use today to develop the hackamore horse, (from left to right) are 3/4", 5/8" and 1/2". The size is determined by the diameter of the side bar of the bosal.

Mechanicals of the Bosal

The nose button is usually braided with a finer braid than used on the bars of the bosal. Its purpose is to rotate on the horse's nose as the bosal is activated through the reins, causing the horse's face to come towards the vertical. That, in turn, stretches the nuchal ligament to open the withers. Neurologically and biomechanically, there's a lot going on through the use of a hackamore, making it an extremely effective tool. A horse's face has more nerves endings in it than the human hand so it is very sensitive to pressure. That sensitivity varies from horse to horse. That's why nose buttons are made in different shapes.

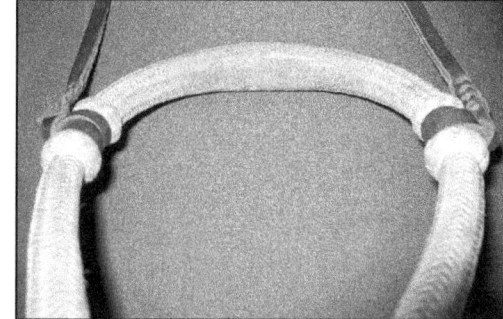

Inside of the flat-shaped nose button. This nose button will move into the horse's face just before it rotates. The rotation will start from the bottom instead of the center like a round-shaped one. This creates a different feel on the horse's nose.

A round nose button will begin its rotation from the center and radiate out to the sides. If this round nose button is made with a bulge in the middle, it will generate more energy. A nose button that is made flat on the inside will move into the face and its rotation will start near the top of the flat area with the energy then radiating out to the sides. It's been my experience that more horses like a round nose button than those that prefer a flat one. Of course, any horse can be ridden in either. But you'll find that the one he likes the best is the one he responds to quicker.

Notes on the Hackamore

1. Used correctly, the hackamore can create three effects:
   Lifting, flexing and direction
   a. The bars produce the lifting effect, lateral flexion and direction.
   b. The nose button produces the vertical flexing effects.
2. When the heel knot is too big, it slows down the action (energy) of the nose button.
3. If the heel knot is too close to the jawbone, the horse becomes dull to the signal.
4. If a hackamore is built based on a 5" spread, the horse becomes dull to the signal because it closes too much to the face and can't create energy to create quickness of response to the signal.
5. Remember, Energy creates Movement.
6. Nose Button creates vertical flexion and creates energy
   a. Short is better (to a point).
7. Hackamore—too close to the sides of the face, i.e., touching, where the head hanger is creates a dull, low level of energy.
8. A braided leather hackamore gives a dull signal because it is too soft with little energy produced.
9. When you come down a size in the bosal or the rope (weight and size), the horse must be as light or lighter as he was in the one you came down from. If he is not, then you must go back up to what you had before. You must also be able to disarm braces or "tests" by the horse in the same amount of time or faster. ("Light" or "lighter" means faster response time to signal.)
10. When doing your finishing work in the 1/2" hackamore, don't use a *mecáte* that is too directional, i.e., too stiff.

The length of the nose button should be from six-to-eight inches when measured on the inside of a bosal that has a six-inch spread between the bars. If the nose button is made too long, it distributes its energy over too wide an area on the horse's nose and slows down the speed of response to the rider's signal. If it is too short, too much of the energy is directed to one spot, and if you are asking for any lateral flexion, most of the time the horse will not tuck his jaw into his neck.

The Heel Knot

The heel knot that holds the bars together contributes weight, along with the reins, for the release of your signals. The size of the heel knot needs to be in relation to the size of the bosal. For example, if the bosal had a 1/2-inch bar size but its heel knot is two inches in diameter, it would be too large and it would overpower the bosal. Upon release of the hand signal, that bosal would put too much weight into the nose button, causing the horse to change the position of his face to either over-vertical or under-vertical.

These three bosals are all 3/4 inch bar size, but each one has a slightly different nose button (from left to right). The first bosal with the coarse braid has a round nose button, the second is a round nose with a slight bulge in the middle and the third is round with a bigger bulge in the middle. The more bulge in the nose button equates to more energy in the signal.

To measure the length of the bosal, the measurement is taken from inside the nose button to the inside of the heel knot. Side-to-side, it should have a six-inch spread between the bars at the hanger knots. Bosals made with narrower spreads, like five inches, were used primarily for braiding fancy art pieces or what is referred to as "fiesta gear." These types of bosals deliver duller signals because the area between the end of the nose button and the head hanger button gets too close to the side of the horse's face, taking some of the movement away from the bosal. Made correctly, the bosal has three effects on the horse: the bars produce a lifting effect, vertical flexion and direction; and the nose button has vertical flexing effects. Anytime the bosal is wrapped tight to the face, all signals become slower and less effective. The leather strap attached to the bosal that's used to hold it on the horse's head like a headstall is called a "hanger." This needs to be made from a light piece of leather or other material in order to remain flexible and supple. If the hanger is constructed from leather that is too heavy, thick or stiff, the rotating action of the nose button will distort and slow the signal between rider and horse.

Each part of the bosal contributes to the horse's understanding of what you are asking. The bars move into the sides of the face to indicate direction. The rotation of the nose button on the nose moves the face towards the vertical, and the heel knot contributes to the release of the signal.

HACKAMORE REINS

The reins used in the hackamore discipline are called ***mecáte***, or rope, and are made of horsehair, either from the mane or tail. Mane hair is much preferred because it is soft and easy on the hands. The horsehair used to make these rope reins are an excellent material because they allow the reins maker to determine the precise weight by how much hair he uses to build the rope. This is an important factor.

Ropes can be made in sizes from one inch in diameter down to a quarter-inch. Normally, the diameter of the rope used is the same size in diameter as the bosal bars.

Twisting the hairs into strands and then twisting a number of strands together is how to get the size rope you want. Ropes are usually made in either four, six or eight strands, and can have a core in the center that the individual strands are twisted around. Ropes can also be made without a core. If a core is used to make a rope, the core is also made of horsehair, which can either be twisted or braided.

As the number of strands increase in a rope of a particular size, the rope will correspondingly increase in weight. For instance, a three-quarter-inch, eight-strand rope will normally weigh about three pounds. A three-quarter-inch, six-strand rope will weigh about two-and-a-half pounds. And a four-strand rope will weigh about two-and-a-quarter pounds.

This progressive reduction in weight continues down through the rope sizes, each time dropping about a quarter pound to a half-pound in weight.

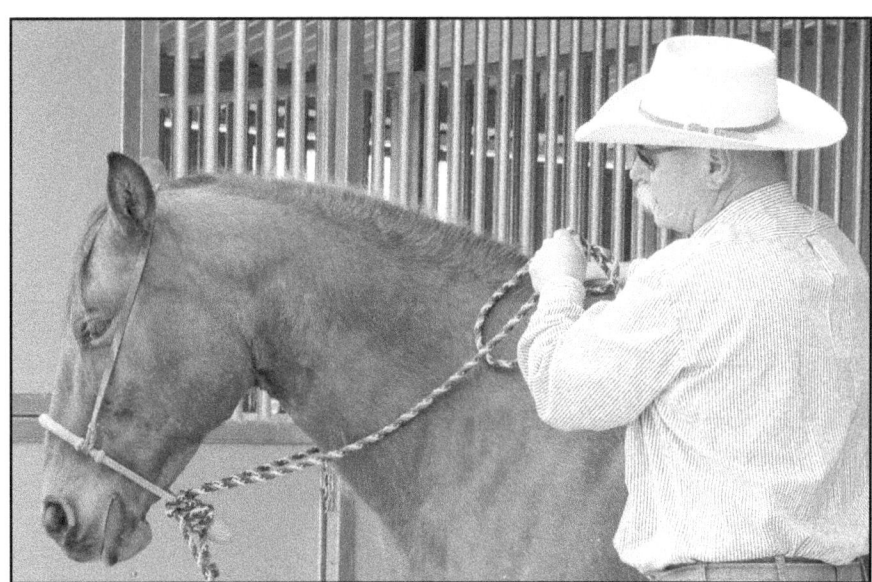

Asking the horse to flex off the nose button.

Lifting effects of the bars of the bosal.

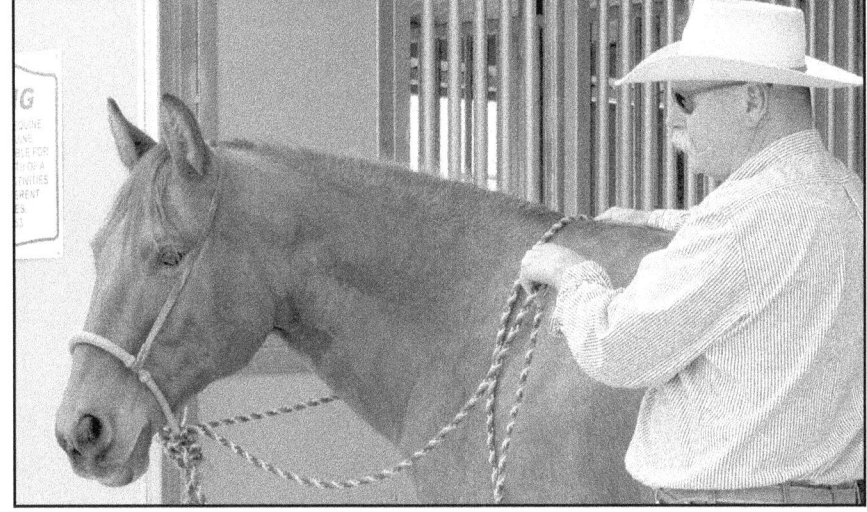

Lateral flexion to the left from the right bar of the bosal. The left rein becomes passive as the horse responds from the ground. The left rein was the first signal and the right rein supports the bend.

Hackamore ropes are usually 22 feet in length so you have plenty of rope to adjust the rein length to your needs and still have rope left over for a lead rope, which is called the "get down" rope.

The three pieces of equipment together—the bosal, the hanger and the horsehair reins—compose what's known as a "hackamore."

BOSAL AND REIN CHANGES TO BUILD A TRUE HACKAMORE HORSE

The different weights of the ropes and the different sizes of bosals are what are used to build the hackamore horse. You can ride any horse in the hackamore but that does not make him a hackamore horse.

A horse that has been ridden in this discipline, and has gone through a series of changes from big bosals and heavy ropes through the mid-size bosals and ropes to the small half-inch bosal and ropes, will have a different carriage than a horse with the same amount of time ridden only in the snaffle bit. A horse ridden correctly through these bosal and rope changes will become lighter in the front end more quickly than a snaffle bit horse, and will have a rounder topline frame from poll to tail. This happens because the bosal has both a lifting effect and a flexing effect as opposed to a snaffle bit that has only a lifting effect. You can flex a horse with a snaffle bit but if you continually keep flexing him, there is a tendency for the horse to get "wadded up" in the neck and work with his face past the vertical which will put more load on his shoulders for him to balance and re-balance.

When I was a kid and young man, we didn't start horses until they were four-to-six years old. They had to be stout enough to be able to make a day's ride. These older horses were started in the 7/8 of an inch or one inch bosal. Now that we start younger horses at two or three years of age, I don't use these bigger bosals to build my hackamore horse.

My style has evolved to where I start with the three-quarter-inch bosal and a rope that weighs from two-and-a-half to three pounds. As my horse develops and shows understanding of the things I'm asking of him, becoming responsive to my signals, I'll reach a point where I think he will answer those same signals with less weight. That's when I'll make a rope change and drop one-quarter pound to a half-pound of weight.

Knowing When to Change

BOSAL AND ROPE CHANGES USED IN SCHOOLING A HORSE IN THE HACKAMORE					
Bosal Size	Bosal Length	Rope Size	Rope Weight	Strands	Time
Measured by diameter of side bars	Measured from inside of Nose Button to inside bottom of Heel Knot, measured with a 6 inch spread between the bars	Mane Hair Mecáte Diameter & Length	Weight in pounds	# of strands	Guideline
3/4"	11 1/2" - 12 1/2"	3/4"	3 lbs	8	@ 3 yrs for this section
3/4" (12 Plait)		3/4" (22 Feet)	2 1/2 lbs	6	
3/4"		5/8"	2-2 1/8 lbs	8	
5/8"	10 1/2" - 11 1/2"	5/8"	2-2 1/8 lbs	8	@ 1 1/2 yrs for this section
5/8" (16 Plait)		5/8" (22 Feet)	1 3/4-2 lbs	6	
5/8"		5/8"	1 1/8-1 1/4 lbs	4	
1/2" (16-18 Plait)	10" - 11 1/2"	1/2" (22 Feet)	1-1 1/8 lbs	4-6	Finishing Work (one handed) @ 1 - 1/2 yrs
1/2"		1/2"	3/4-7/8 lbs	4	
3/8 - 5/16" (Two Rein Bosal)	9" - 10 1/2"	3/8 (22 Feet) 5/16"	N/A	4	

NOTE: Nose button should be 6" - 8" long, measured along the inside edge, with the bars spread 6" apart.
Credits: Information source: Mike Bridges (http://mikebridges.net)
Document Design & Format Source: Jim Reilly (http://jimreilly.net)

When I make the change to a lighter rope, the horse needs to be as good or better than he was in the heavier rope. That means that he responds faster to my hand signals. When he braces or resists from lack of balance, or is testing my program, I can disarm him as quickly as I could with the heavier rope. If he does not, I'll go back to the heavier rope and do more work. I might have 30-to-50 rides on him before the change; however long it takes. Each horse is different.

In the second rope, I'll do more work in the exercises I'm using at this stage of development. Again, when I think he can respond as good or better to the signals, I'll step down to a 2 3/8 to 2 5/8 pound rope while still using a 3/4-inch bosal.

At this point if I have been using a bosal that has a 12-plait braided bar, I will change to one that has a 16- or 18-plaited bar. This produces a finer signal because the smaller braid has less bite when it touches the side of his face. If my progress is consistent, I should be able to get the same or better response from the horse by asking with less signal. I do more development at the same weight rope. The next change I make will be to the 5/8-inch bosal with a 16- or 18-plait braided bar and rope that weighs 2-to-2 1/8 pounds.

In this 5/8 inch bosal, I will also make three rope changes. I begin with the 2-to-2 1/8 pound rope and finish with a rope that weighs 1 1/8-to-1 1/4 pounds.

Finish Work

By now, I've been riding this horse for two or three years. He is well balanced and can do the movements I need to work cattle with quality. At this stage, I am ready for the finish work in the hackamore.

Finish work is getting the last elements of balance and achieving the ultimate "speed-to-signal" for this particular horse to attain a high level of performance with the least amount of weight in the hackamore. "Speed-to-signal" is the horse's response time to the hand and body signals delivered by the rider. I, personally, never deliver a hand signal without delivering a body signal, and am continually looking for the horse to get faster and faster in response time.

My next change is to the 1/2-inch bosal with a rope weighing about one pound to 1 1/8 pounds. I keep asking him to become lighter. The last rope I use for the finish work is a rope that weighs from 3/4 of a pound to 7/8 of a pound.

This is the way I learned to build a hackamore horse. It takes time and a lot of good riding. There is a reason for all these changes. There will come a point during this training at which the horse will develop what's known as "self-carriage." The old-timers I grew up with used to say that is when the horse is "working inside the bosal."

This means that as I am asking the hips of the horse to push forward under his body, or engage, and I am holding a supporting rein to the hackamore (passive light contact), the horse brings his head toward—or at—the vertical to open his withers to match the amount of engagement of the hips without the rider asking by changing his hands.

The horse at this stage is achieving self-carriage because of his willingness to take more weight over the hindquarters, committing his loin and engaging the hip, thereby allowing the shoulders to elevate. This immediately makes the shoulders much more mobile. For cow work, this is extremely important.

When I was a young man in my twenties, there was a time I thought the old-timers were wrong. I figured that there had to be a faster way to make a hackamore horse. I wanted to get these horses into the bridle. So I started a lot of horses in the 5/8-inch bosal and a few in the 1/2-inch bosal. I made some real nice horses, but none of them ever developed self-carriage. I always had to ask them to come into my hands when I started pushing the hip forward if I wanted some degree of collection.

Asking a horse to "come into your hands" is changing from a passive rein back to having contact with the face of the horse. It requires a shortening of the passive rein until you feel the hackamore or snaffle bit in your hands. At that point, you have contact with the face. Beyond that point, the next step in contact is a change in the face from contact toward the vertical.

This ability of the horse to achieve self-carriage will make things a lot easier as I transfer him to one hand when I start into the two-rein process. It turns out the old-timers were right. If you want your horse to reach the highest levels of this discipline, you have to take the time.

FINDING RELEASE FROM PRESSURE

Mentally for the horse, with all of the signals coming from the bosal, I am asking that he release himself from pressure. For instance, if I move the left rein to ask the horse to move in that direction, the right bar of the bosal moves into the side of his face. Going to the right, it would be the left bar of the bosal. The nose button rotates on the nose and the face yields in toward the vertical. I can modify signals that are already applied by adding a "tug" to the hand signal, telling the horse I want more movement. I can rotate the nose button by adding a little "bump" sideways with my hand while still holding the original signal.

A "tug" is a lateral movement of the forearm rein hand with no break in the wrist to bring more of the bar into the side of the face or into the jawbone of the horse. A "bump" is a lateral move of the rein hand but with a break in the wrist at the moment of movement. And a bump can be added to either the direct rein or the indirect rein whereas the tug would be added only to the direct rein.

> **Hand Positions on the Hackamore**
>
> 1. Rotation of the nose button: Close hands first. If no response, then, with knuckles up or "canted," move wrist only laterally with a little "bump."
>
> 2. Move side bars: With knuckles up slightly, move forearm laterally with no break in wrist. This is a "tug."
>
> 3. Create a turn with the horse by holding your hand with knuckles up and swinging forearm laterally, keeping elbow close to waist/hip area and "driving" with outside leg.

As stated before, I would generally use a rope rein that is the same size diameter as the bar of the bosal. The reason is because to get it to operate correctly it takes so much hair to create the weight needed to match the bosal size. If I took a 3/4-inch bosal and used a 1/2-inch hair rope on it, there would not be enough weight to get the best action and response communicated to the horse. And if I used a three-quarter-inch hair rope on a 1/2-inch bosal, I would overpower the bosal, making it too heavy in the nose. In time, that would make the horse dull to the signal.

This is not a discipline of power. Horses don't work well when made to do things by brute force. The hackamore is used with finesse. The heavier rope at the start merely puts more energy into my signals. Despite this, the horse is going to test the program with little braces and resistances. This is natural.

That's the same as when he tests other horses in his herd to gain or hold social position.

The heavier ropes and bigger bosals give me more weight and bearing surface to help answer those braces. As he answers my signals with more fluid movement and less brace, we are then ready to ask him to respond with less weight.

SPEED OF THE SIGNALS

I have a lot of latitude in adjusting the speed of my signals. The farther the bars of the bosal are from the sides of the horse's face, the slower the signal. Some horses need this more than others at the beginning of the training. If I tie the hackamore so the bars are a 1/2-inch off of the horse's face on each side, this creates a very slow signal for him. He will feel the movement of the bosal before the bar touches the side of his face, giving him time to prepare mentally for the movement. If the bars are up against the side of the horse's face, then I have created an extremely fast signal. At the start of the training, most horses do not have the balance to respond to that fast of a signal without a brace, which will create resistance.

> **Bosal Length and Number of Mecáte Wraps**
>
> 1. The correct number of wraps (after the 1st half-wrap) is from one to four, with two or three preferred. This should leave one or two fingers width space between the horse's jawbone and the "whooie" knot.
>
> 2. You can have the mecáte wrap touching horse's jawbone hair, i.e., no finger space between jawbone and "whooie" knot (for a short time) if horse is "testing" your hand, i.e., pushing through it.
>
> 3. The bosal will be too long if you have more than four full wraps of the mecáte (after the first half-wrap) around the bosal plus the reins and the "whooie" knot.
>
> 4. You can try to reduce the number of wraps (if more than four) by using a wine bottle cork to plug the bottom of the bosal at the heel knot and then start wrapping the mecáte.
>
> 5. Too many wraps (more than four) overpowers the nose button and pulls it into the horse's face before it rotates; then the horse pushes his face into it to seek relief which has the exact opposite effect from what you want.

As I get more understanding from the horse, I speed up the signal by bringing the bars closer to the face by tightening the "whooie" knot on the reins. And, in the end, the bars can be next to the face, which creates a very fast signal. When the bars are tight to the horse's face, the nose button area of the bosal, from the hanger forward, cannot be tight on the face or it will lose a lot of the energy in the signal. The bosal will become "dead" and my signals will be dull. This is the major reason I want my bosals made with a six inch spread between the bars.

A lot of horses need some time between when I start the rein moving and when the bar touches the side of the face in order to get mentally prepared to respond. This can be only fractions of a second in time, but it can be important. Most of my horses spend three-to-four years being ridden in the hackamore.

TYING THE REINS TO THE BOSAL

There are a number of ways to tie the ***mecáte*** to the bosal. I use a way that is very fast and easy. This is important because when you are through using it, it should be untied and removed from your bosal each day. If it's left tied over a long period of time, the bars of the bosal will become distorted and change the rotation of the nose button.

To put the reins on, hold the bosal in your left hand with the nose button towards your body. Wedge the knotted end of the rope into the bosal at the heel knot.

Then wrap the rope around the bosal, either away from you or toward you. It's your choice. The wraps should be snug but not tight. You don't want to bend the bars of the bosal inward.

You can use one to four wraps around the outside of the bosal before pulling the reins through, but no more. Five or more wraps begin to create too much heel weight. The number of wraps you need will depend on the size of the horse's face and the length of your bosal. A larger-muzzled horse will require fewer wraps in order for the bosal to fit over his nose with the proper spacing.

Next, reach through the bars of the bosal to pull your rope back through. Keep pulling the rope until you get the rein length you want. Then drop the reins behind the heel knot. At this point, take the twist out of your rope. Get ahold of the free end of the rope with your palm up and then rotate your hand so that your thumb points to your navel. At this point, the rope crosses itself. Put the nose button of the bosal through the loop that you've just created and then drop it on the bars of the bosal back by your wraps. Get the free end of the rope and pull your knot down snug. You are now ready to place it on your horse and ride.

TYING THE MECÁTE

1 Place knotted end of rope into the bosal at the heel knot.

Tying the Mecáte, continued

2

Put your wraps around the bosal, either away from you or towards you (your choice). Put them on snug but not tight.

3

Three or four wraps before starting your reins. If you have to use five or more wraps your bosal is too long and you will create too much heel weight.

4

Reach through the bars of the bosal and get a hold of your rope and pull it back through.

5 Keep pulling the rope and measure your rein length after you have the length you want, drop it behind the heel knot.

Tying the Mecáte, continued

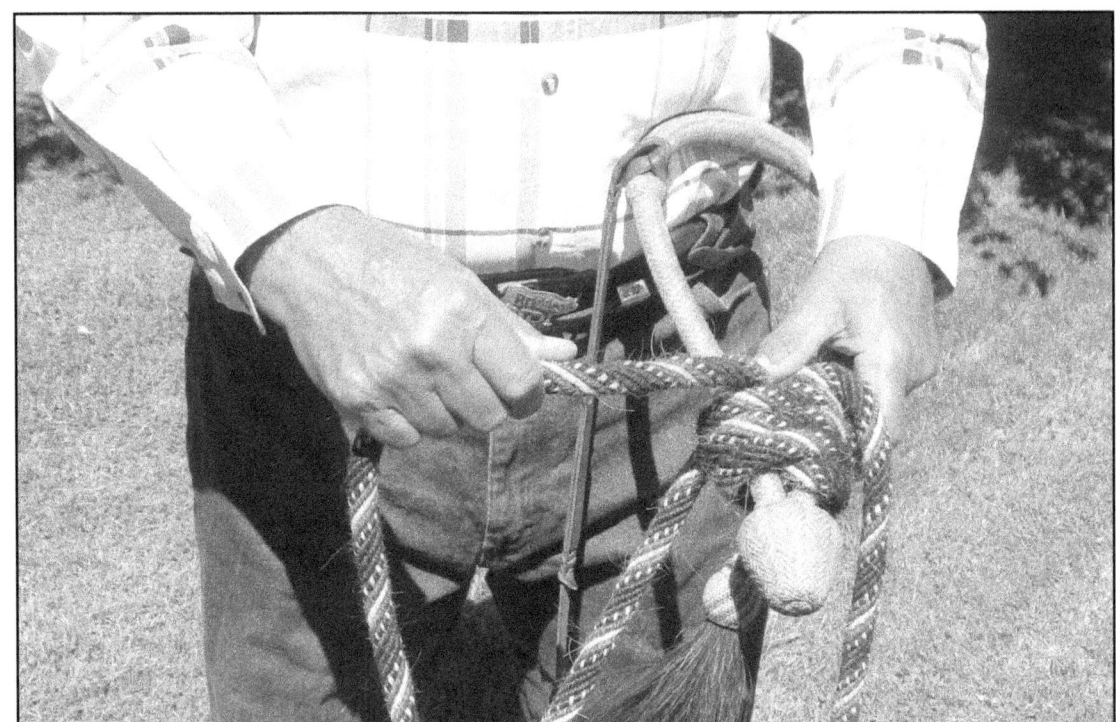

6 | Take the twist out of your rope.

7

Reach and get the lead end of the rope and place it in your hand with your palm up.

8 Turn your palm toward your body. Note that the rope crosses itself.

9 Put the nose of the bosal through the loop that you have created and then drop it on the bars of the bosal back by your wraps.

10 Reach and get the lead end of the rope and pull knot down snug.

Tying the Mecáte, continued

You are Ready to Ride

Chapter 3

Introducing the Hackamore to the Young Horse

When I first hang a hackamore on a new horse, I don't know where the "sweet spot" is but want to find it. The sweet spot is the area of the horse's nose where he will respond the quickest to my signals. It will take about one-to-three rides to find it by moving the bosal up and down the face in little increments. Its placement may differ with each horse.

When I locate it for that particular horse, that's where I'll hang the bosal for most of our work. If I'm going to ride my horse for periods of two hours or more, I'll need to adjust the hanger to move the bosal up or down from the sweet spot to give it a rest. I want this area to stay "bright" or responsive. The rest time only needs to be 10-to-20 minutes, then I re-adjust the hanger to put the bosal back to the sweet spot.

Some horses develop a bald spot on their nose where the hair will rub off. Other horses won't lose any hair. This has something to do with the density of the hair follicles. When you see a bald spot, it doesn't necessarily mean that the horse's nose is sore. If the hackamore is used correctly, it will not sore or skin up any part of the face. To find the proper place, I'll adjust the hanger so the bosal is around the middle of the face between the eyes and the nostrils. There should be a slight angle from the nose button to the heel knot. The heel knot should always hang lower than the nose button, even when the reins are activated and all the slack is removed when riding.

If you place the bosal too high on the nose, you'll lose sensitivity. If you place it too low on the nose, the heel knot will be higher than the nose button when you activate the bosal with a hand signal, and that's incorrect. This will cause the bottom of the nose button to pull into the face. If this continues, over a short period of time the horse will start to push against the bosal. I never want my horse to learn that he can push through the bosal or my hands. Instead, I want the opposite—response without resistance.

Highest position of the nose button on the horses face.

Lowest position of the nose button that might still be correct. You are looking for the position or spot on the nose where the horse responds the fastest to the signals. For most horses it will be someplace between the highest and the lowest spots.

You are now below the nose cartilage and the heel knot at the end of the signal will get higher than the nose button. This causes the nose button to pull into the horse's face. The horse will immediately resist.

Mentally, it's helpful for a horse if I first do some groundwork. It helps him understand the signals coming from the bosal even before I ride him. I'm not after quality of movement, merely an understanding of the bosal's bar signals and rotation of the nose button.

To begin this simple exercise, I shorten my hackamore reins so they go from the bosal over the neck of the horse, behind the poll area, down the other side of the neck and back to the bosal. This gives me a much longer lead rope to work with and prevents the bosal from pulling off his nose if he makes a hard move.

Standing at his shoulders, I put one hand on the shoulder to help support him. With my other hand, I move the rein, which is the long "get down rope," so the opposite bar moves into the side of his face. I want to see him move his face away from the pressure and toward me but not move his body. He needs only to move his head a little.

I then straighten his head back to center and repeat until he starts to move toward me at the first touch of the bar to his face. I then switch to the other side and get the same behavior established there. Remember to have the bosal open so the bars are not tight to the face. I want a slow signal at this point.

When I see that my horse understands, I go back to the first side I worked. Standing just behind the left eye of the horse, I pass the lead rope over his head and down the right side of his body. I pass it behind the cantle of the saddle and back to my hand, and then I take the slack out of the rope on the right side of the horse. Next, I move the horse's face off-center to the right and give a little pull on the rope, moving the left bar of the bosal against his face as the horse turns.

Before he gets about halfway around, I create a little energy in the rope around his hip so that he goes a little forward as he is turning. As he reaches the halfway point of the turn-around, I move slightly to the right so the horse sees me with his right eye. When I'm in his vision, I start backing up so he keeps coming forward four-to-six straight steps. I repeat this three or four times.

When I see him beginning to understand, I start the turnaround with his head straight on his body. A total of six-to-eight turns are usually enough. Then I'm ready for the other side. Normally, I'm going to find one side that takes more signal to operate than the other. My earlier groundwork will tell me which side of the horse has more resistance, so I need to be prepared.

I don't want to overpower the horse. I just want to be ready to add a little more signal the instant I feel him brace, or resist. Timing is important. If I can answer—or respond to—the brace when it's starting, the horse will give it up faster.

I do this exercise only three or four times before I ride him. After that, he doesn't need it. On the third session for the turnaround, I will put my rope over the seat of my saddle instead of around the cantle. This brings the rope to a higher angle that is more like a hand signal.

To finish the exercise, I lengthen the reins as if I'm going to ride him. I stand at the horse's shoulder. I hold a rein in each hand with all my fingers closed on both sides of his neck just ahead of the front fork of the saddle. Then I ask the horse to "come to my hands." That means he should yield his face without dropping his poll. The reins need to be short enough so I can feel the bosal through the reins.

The first signal is to close my hands. This will rotate the nose button slightly. The horse's face should move towards vertical. If the horse does not respond, I then rotate the nose button by adding a lateral bump with one hand. This bump needs to be a sideways—not backward—move of the hand in a horizontal position knuckles up, coming from the wrist, not the arm. Should I need to do it more than once, and I will at the beginning, I'll alternate the bumps from one hand to the other with a slight pause between bumps, with each bump having slightly more intensity. When the horse responds by moving his face in toward his chest, I open my hands and release him. Then I ask him again. I do this enough times until he starts to move his face when I close my hands.

When the face comes in, the reins will become light in my hands, but I'll still have contact with the bosal. Now I'll ask him to hold that position with softness for two or three seconds and then release him. I do that three or four times. Then I ask him to move his head laterally right and left. If I asked him to move it to the right, I would move my right rein hand laterally to the right. If I was sitting on the horse, at the same moment I moved my hand, I would move my lower right leg ahead of the 14th thoracic vertebra in his back to help influence the lateral movement. The movement of the right hand would move the left bar of the hackamore into the side of the horse's face, which would ask him to bend laterally to the right. If I rode him, the influence of the leg would create some contraction to the oblique and abdominal muscles on the right side of the horse, helping to contribute to right lateral flexion. To the left would be the reverse of those signals.

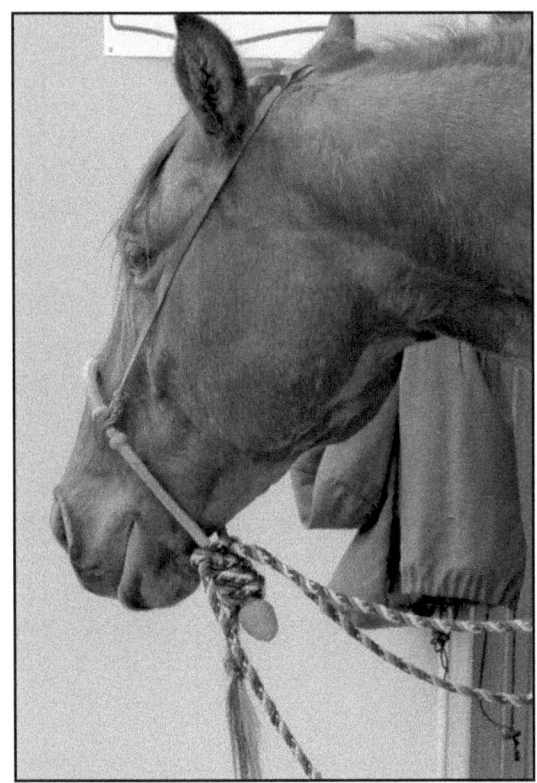

The bosal hanging on the face is in the correct position for this horse. The mecáte reins are tied with four wraps. With the four wraps and then the whooie knot, this horse will respond better with a fair amount of heel weight. Also notice that the head hanger is inside-out. This bosal is starting to get too much heel down bend to it. So, I will tie it from the other side till it gets straight again.

Some horses want to back up when I begin this nose rotation work. I just back with them but continue to ask them to move their faces and release them when they do. If they have trouble understanding what I'm asking them, I will position them close to a wall so they see a barrier behind them in their peripheral vision.

THE FIRST RIDE IN THE HACKAMORE

My goal during the first ride in the hackamore is for the horse to understand and be respectful of my hand signals as they pertain to the different parts of the bosal; the bar signals, rotation of the nose button and the release of the signals. I'm also going to introduce some new body signals, primarily my leg influence to the mid-body of the horse.

It's important that I encourage my horse to go forward from the hindquarters and not pull from the forequarters, regardless of the gait. When I ask him to go backward, I think to myself, "Go forward in the opposite direction," which means I want him to start to drive from his hips, only moving backward. In introducing new things to the horse, where he is trying to sort things out, it is very easy for a rider to forget about keeping the life, or energy, up in the horse. The more life you have in the gait, the quicker you will get understanding from the horse of your signals and the less energy it will take when you apply the signal.

I like to work my horse in a big circle, somewhere between 60 and 80 feet for this work. If I have a round pen, that's great because the barriers can be helpful. If not, then I work in an open area.

FORWARD ON A SUPPORTING REIN

To start, I ask the horse to move forward at the walk on a supporting rein to establish my circle. A supporting rein means no signal to the horse but some contact with the bosal. When I feel that he's comfortable, I'll shorten my reins so I have contact, meaning I can feel the bosal and have a firm influence to his face. I'll ride him like this for five or six strides and then go back to a supporting rein. After two or three times of that, I'll change directions and repeat supporting rein to contact rein.

My next step is to ask for some lateral flexion. If I'm going clockwise to the right on my circle, I'll move my right hand laterally away from the horse. This causes the left bar of the

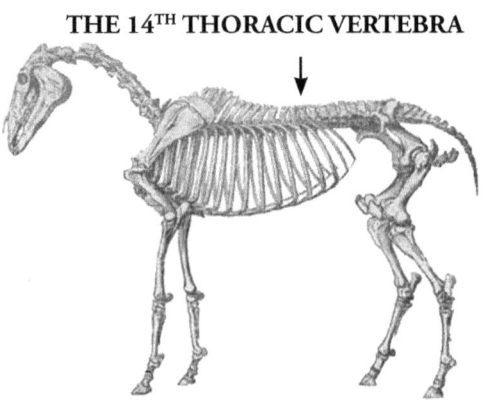

THE 14TH THORACIC VERTEBRA

hackamore to move to the left side of the horse's face, causing him to tip his face to the right. At the same instant, or even momentarily before I start my hand signal, I'll put the calf muscle of my right leg on the horse's body ahead of the 14th thoracic vertebra, which I'll refer to as the "14th."

Right from the start, I want the horse to bend laterally from the poll all the way through his mid-body. I don't want him to bend only from the base of his neck. I use my other leg on the outside of the bend (going to the right, my left leg) to ask the horse to move forward. To do this, I use the lower part of my leg below the calf to create energy behind the 14th. Whenever I put bend, or arc, in my horses' bodies, I drive them forward with my outside leg by creating energy in that leg. Actually, the way I think of it is that I drive them forward 97 percent with my outside leg and three percent with the inside leg.

Because I'm going to work cattle with my horse, I want the energy coming from his body to radiate into the bend or arc so that the cow will feel his power. The turns I will need to develop to control and dominate cattle require the horse to turn in a very small area, often less than the length of his body. It is much easier for the horse to make these kinds of turns when the energy is moving from the outside of the bend to the inside, much like spinning a top.

When the horse answers, or responds, to the left bar of the bosal and moves his head to the right, I will soften my hand and my leg signals. After a couple of strides, I will release the hand signal and release the leg, letting him go five-to-seven strides before asking again. Each time I ask I will start the hand signal from "home base."

Home base is where all signals should start from and it is where I hold my hands when riding. It's the area right in front of the fork of my saddle, two-to-three inches above the horse's mane. As I signal the horse, I'll move one hand or the other outward laterally until the horse finds the signal. As my hand moves farther from home base, I also increase the leg influence by adding the Achilles tendon with a slight vertical stroke to the horse's oblique muscles.

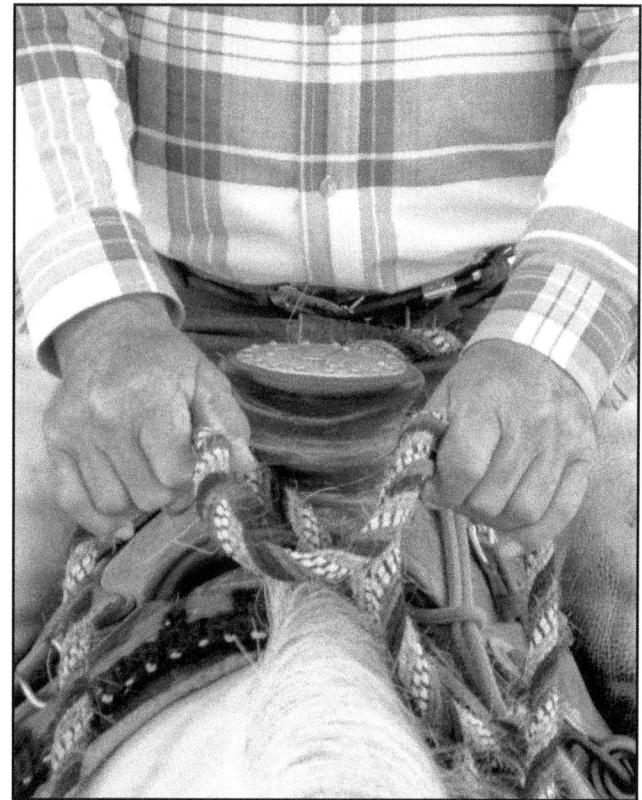

Home base for your hands.

I'll keep working on one side of the horse until I get some understanding and he can go forward a few strides with a slight bend from the poll through to the 14th while maintaining his line of travel along the arc of the big circle. I always give the horse a release between each set of lateral flexions, allowing him to travel unbent a few more strides than when he was bent. The release given to the horse at this point is not abandonment of signals but to allow the rein to lengthen gradually as he goes forward, not just throwing the reins away.

When I feel that he's ready to change directions, I will create some bend in his body and take him off the line of the circle through the middle to go the other way, repeating the same steps until I have some understanding; two or three strides without any brace in his body. A brace is a resistance in the muscle or group of muscles any place in the horse's body that interferes with the flow of movement or the alignment of structures.

Social Braces and Training Braces

There are two types of braces: social and training braces. Social braces are the ones that come about when the horse is going to test the program. He would like to be one rung higher than me on his social ladder. I ask something of him and he wants to do it his way, not my way, or doesn't want to do it at all.

Training braces come about as I am teaching new movements to the horse and he doesn't have the ability to maintain balance throughout the movement. He will brace different parts of his body in order to get through the movement. In doing this, he will create resistances. As his balance and strength improves, the resistances diminish.

Both kinds of braces need to be addressed. Training braces can take longer to remove completely because the horse has to achieve balance and the ability to re-balance through the movement. That only comes about with good riding, recognizing where the brace is coming from and knowing what needs to move to get it to release.

If my horse braces against my signals, then I need to hold my signal longer and add intensity to it until he releases the brace. As soon as he gives up the brace, I will release him, go a few steps and ask again.

I don't want to release a signal while a horse is bracing against it. More than likely at first, my horse will continue to give me little tests, either in his face or body, or both. This is natural. I'll need to answer them but won't want to overpower him. I'll just add enough energy or movement in my signals so that he gives them up. At this stage of development, my release is his reward for giving up the brace. Later on, I won't release him but will merely soften my hand and leg when he gives up the brace but continue to hold the signals.

After the second side is where I want it, I will go back to the first side and do some more work until I can get at least five strides with the horse staying on line with a slight lateral flexion without brace. Then I return to the second side again and repeat until that side is equal.

Coming to Vertical

Now that I have the horse's understanding of the bosal bar signals, I'm ready to start on rotation of the nose button to develop his vertical flexion. I'm going to ask my horse to yield to, or "come off," the nose button of the bosal all the way to vertical with his face. I know this much flexion will be more than is necessary for the amount of engagement the horse can achieve with his hindquarters at this stage of training. My purpose is that right from the start I want this horse to learn that he must be respectful of my hands. When I ask him to come back into my hands from a passive rein, he needs to instantly respond without resistance.

When gathering cattle, driving cattle or just riding across the countryside, I spend long periods of time riding my horses on a passive rein without any contact to the face through the reins. When I need to do something that requires some openness in the back, I need to be able to get contact with the face without resistance so I can bring the face toward the vertical or at the vertical for the amount of openness I need at the withers.

A lot of that work doesn't require his face to be all the way to vertical. As I get into the next stage of development work, I'll be in no hurry to close the angle of his face. As his hips begin to be able to drive farther under the mass of his body with a lifting or carrying energy, his mid-back will open, or rise, and his withers should match that openness.

> ### What is "Shortening of the Base?"
> The "base" of the horse is the overall length of the horse, measured from where his hind feet are placed on the ground to the tip of his nose.
>
> Shortening of the base is when the back end of the horse—the hips—get closer to the front end of the horse—the face.
>
> By signal, influence and drive, I ask the horse's pelvis to come to a tilted position which puts the stifle joint more forward and the hind legs of the horse underneath the mass of the body more. This is referred to as "engagement."
>
> This process contracts the abdominal and oblique muscles more than they previously were. This, in turn, allows the major muscle groups in the back, along with the supraspinous ligament, to extend themselves so that the spinous processes can separate themselves.
>
> As this is happening, the base of the neck pushes up into the shoulders, lifting the withers, shortening the antagonist muscles between the neck and back, which brings the face toward the vertical. Depending on how much engagement I have created from the hip forward will determine what degree of collection I have created.

All this takes time and work to develop. For our little exercise in this first ride in the hackamore, I will bring him all the way to the vertical so that mentally he learns that he can be obedient to a combination of signals.

With my horse going forward in a big circle, I will shorten my passive rein until I have passive contact with the bosal. My first signal to rotate the nose button is to simply close, or tighten, my hands around the reins. If my horse doesn't respond with a change in the angle of his face, I will spread my hands laterally four-to-five inches and, at the same time, put more power into my grip on the reins. If there is still no response, I will add in a lateral bump, the same as in the ground preparation. I'll keep bumping until the face changes towards the vertical, and then release him back to passive contact. I'll ride six or seven strides and ask again.

As I start the first hand signal—the closing of my hands—I will put the calf muscles of both my legs onto my horse. This is to ask for some contraction of the oblique and abdominal muscles of the horse. As these muscles contract, it changes the base of the neck to help to bring the horse's head and face toward the vertical. If I add more intensity to my hand signals, I add more to my leg signals. Whenever a horse responds and I release my hands, I also release the legs.

When the horse starts to find it, I ask him to hold it for two strides with softness. When that gets good, I then go to three strides, building up to five strides. I always remember to give him time to relax, but keep going forward. When he is going forward without resistance, I remember to soften my signals to match his softness. When I do release my signals, I make sure it is when he is soft, and not on a brace.

> ## Weight, Pressure or Energy of My Signals
> ### Feathers, Wood or Iron
>
> The lightness of feathers: hummingbird, robin, eagle
> The firmness of wood: balsa, pine, oak
> The strength of iron: ultimate power
>
> I think of the power of my signals in concepts. In riding my horse, the lightest signal would be feathers. Within that concept, the lightest of feathers would be the hummingbird. If my horse responds to my signal that is the weight of a robin's feather, as opposed to the weight of an eagle's feather, he is considerably lighter.
>
> If my horse adds resistance in response to my lightest signal, I would need to increase the pressure of my signal from feathers to wood. The weight of the wood—balsa, pine or oak—would depend upon the amount of his resistance.
>
> If the weight of oak in my signal does not release his brace, I would then have to go to the weight of iron. Now I am at a point beyond finesse, and I would immediately need to have enough power in my signal to get an immediate positive response from the horse.
>
> But as soon as he responds, I need to immediately go back to the weight of feathers.
>
> The amount of pressure I need in my signals is something that is constantly changing through the riding of the horse. This is true whether I am schooling or doing my work.
>
> As time goes on, you will have to go to iron less and less. The return to feathers will be to a lighter-weight feather.

THE CONCEPT OF FEATHERS, WOOD, IRON

I always want to ride with the lightness of feathers in my hands and my body at some point in the development of this bridle horse. If I ever hope to obtain that lightness, I have to offer it to the horse each time I start a signal with my hands and body. If my horse gives back resistance to those signals, I will immediately match his brace with greater intensity. More intensity I equate with wood. The most intensity I equate with iron. The least intensity is feathers. The instant the brace is gone, I need to go back to feathers. This training is important and, for us riders, it takes practice and time to get good. We need to be as fast as we can be, but none of us are fast enough compared to the horse.

Combining Vertical and Lateral Flexion

When I am ready to ask him to change his face to vertical while holding a little lateral flexion, I prefer to start this work while going forward on a circle. I create a little lateral flexion using my inside leg and inside hand signal. My outside leg is the primary driving leg and my outside rein is supporting and maintaining the bend. After a few strides, I increase the power to my inside hand. At the same time, I increase the inside leg influence. When I get the change in his face toward the vertical, I soften my signals and ask him to hold it for a few strides and then release. I keep building to more strides, and work both sides of the horse.

At this stage of the session, my horse has worked enough so that he will want to slow down. When I feel this change, I will offer him the stop by using my body signals; pelvis, back and legs. I'll want light contact with his face through the reins to the nose button of the hackamore.

Asking the horse to flex right with direct rein influence.

When he stops, I will hold the stop signals on him and hug the lower part of his mid-body with my lower legs until he moves one leg back. Then I will release my legs but not the contact with the nose button and face of the horse. I'll put the legs back onto his body and ask for another leg to move backward. After three or four steps on the last release of the legs, I will move my lower legs back toward his hips to ask him to move forward.

I want my horse to learn to back up from my body signals, not from my pulling on his face. I use the bosal only to help him hold his frame through the stop and after the stop into the back up. If my horse needs some help finding the stop and backing up, then I can put a little backward pressure into the reins. That will pull the nose button into the face of the horse to set up more of a block for his forward energy. If I help him with more nose button pressure from the bosal than the original amount of contact, it becomes an enhancing signal, not the primary signal for the stop or back up.

What is Lateral Flexion?

Lateral flexion in the horse is creating bend through his body from the poll through the neck and ribs to the 14th thoracic vertebra, and having the hips stay in alignment or move into alignment with the shoulders for him to be in correct balance.

The maximum amount the horse can bend laterally is when the outside eye reaches the inside point of the opposite shoulder. As soon as he passes that point, he is overbent. When a horse is overbent, it changes the balance line from down the spine to the outside diagonal which creates a balance line of inside-hip-to-outside-shoulder. That causes the outside shoulder to push away from the movement. This makes it very difficult for the horse to go forward into the bend you've created without brace in his body because you've taken away his arc balance.

Lateral flexion is used in all degrees, from very little flexion to maximum flexion depending on the amount of bend we need in the horse to complete a movement. For the cow horse, bend is something that we always have to create, release and re-create so we can put the horse in a position to dominate the cow. This is especially true at the early stages of training.

Asking the horse to flex left with direct rein influence.

Asking for left flexion with minimal direct rein influence.

Vertical flexion with hands at home base.

Right lateral flexion along with vertical flexion with minimal hands signals.

Vertical flexion, left bend in the horse's body, along with minimal hand signals. The horse has moved his left rib away from the rider's inside leg. The rider's right leg is back far enough to contain the horse's hip.

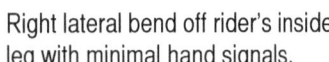

Right lateral bend off rider's inside leg with minimal hand signals.

Left lateral bend off the rider's inside leg with minimal hand signals.

TEACH AT THE WALK, SCHOOL AT THE TROT

I do this first hackamore work at the walk and slow trot, not the canter. The understanding that I establish in this first session will be carried forward the same way for three-to-five more sessions. After the second or third session, I'll do this same work but on a straight line instead of in a circle. Also, I'll ask the horse to make the transition from walk to slow trot while holding both lateral flexion and vertical flexion.

By the end of the fourth or fifth session, my horse should be able to hold these flexions for 20 or more strides. Usually at some point in the second session, I'll start to ask the horse to give me these flexions while standing still. I'll use the same signals as when he has motion in his body. Remember, I don't ask him to hold these flexions for too long to start with. Build up the time. Instead of asking him to hold for so many strides, ask him to hold it for so many seconds. I want him to understand that even when standing still, I can change his frame and that he can hold it. Later in his training, this will be of great value.

Chapter 4

DEVELOPMENT WORK IN THE HACKAMORE: THE EXERCISES

RIDING INSIDE AND OUTSIDE

My basic groundwork establishes good mental understanding in the horse and develops some trust and respect between us. My three-to-five sessions of riding him with the hackamore has shown that the signals from the different parts of the hackamore are understood and he is respectful of my hands. I am now ready to move on.

I like to use a combination of riding outside in the open country with only nature's barriers and riding inside in corrals, pens and arenas. Prior to the time I started to teach this discipline in clinics, 98 percent of my riding and training of my horses was done in the outside country. I worked my horses while I did my job of tending cattle. Now, it's reversed so that 70 percent of my training is done inside some type of man-made structure like a pen, arena or barn.

What I found is that I, rather than my horse, had to make the bigger mental adjustment to this environmental change. My program and style still worked. The same things in the same steps have to be there. But I had to learn how to be creative to build the horse's muscle and tendon strength that naturally would have occurred if all the riding was done outside.

At the same time, I had to keep the horse from becoming bored. My 30 percent outside riding is now very important to me as time to clean up the mind and to give my horse long lines of travel over uneven ground. This gives him lots of opportunities for rebalancing, an important component to this training.

> **The Use and Size of Circles**
>
> You cannot do too much work on circles in the development of the cow horse. I use circles of varying sizes throughout his schooling to develop strength and balance in arc.
>
> The size of the circle needed at any particular time varies greatly depending on the ability of the individual horse and the level of his schooling at that moment. Choosing the size is a judgment call by the rider who must recognize where that horse is mentally and physically for his ability to maintain balance.
>
> In this book, I refer to circles as big, mid-size (or moderate) and small.
>
> - A big circle is 40-to-100 feet in diameter or larger.
> - Mid-size circles are 20-to-40 feet in diameter.
> - Small circles are under 20 feet in diameter.
>
> The size of the circle that's used is constantly being adjusted and depends on the rider's ability to read where his horse is physically and mentally.
>
> Consequently, throughout the book, I won't always state the precise size of the circle needed to school the movement.

Developing Body Strength within the Young Horse

Over the next three or four months of riding, my primary focus is to develop strength throughout the horse's back and legs. The old-timers used to say that it took a year for a horse to learn how to pack the rider. I now believe a horse not only learns to adjust and re-balance while carrying the rider's weight but this period of time is needed to build the strength in his body to be able to accomplish it.

To develop strength in a young horse, I trot him lots of miles at slow and moderate speeds, with short periods at the lengthened trot. Most of those miles are ridden on a passive rein. Occasionally, I'll ask the horse to yield his face toward the vertical a little bit, or, as I like to say, come into my hands. But I don't ask him to yield all the way to vertical.

I want the horse to stretch and lengthen his body, to move forward in a relaxed way, to learn to take the change of terrain in stride, to hold the speed I ask of him, and not to move into a speed that he may want to go.

Accomplishing this takes lots of straight-line work and lots of big circles, from 40- to 80 feet in diameter. I don't think you can ride too many circles in a horse's life. Circles are very important for developing a bridle horse. I also do lots of speed changes within the trot. I ask him to maintain the trot but to travel faster or slower. You should develop the signals between you and your horse needed to do this. Make sure he is driving from the hips, or hindquarters, forward, whether on a circle or on a straight line.

The Start of Lope Work

It's at this point of development that I add lope work. I begin with small amounts, interspersed with the trot work. As he progresses, I add more time to the lope work. I ask for the lope from the outside of the horse's body with my leg behind the 14th. The first stroke of the lope is the outside hind leg striking off. At a moderate speed, I let the slow lope develop by having the horse hunt for it. The horse will try to maintain the lope with the least amount of energy. If I match the rhythm of the gait with my body, he will come to a point and start to slow down as that happens. So I change my rhythm to match his slower pace. In time, he will seek the slower pace on his own because it requires less energy of him. I can always drive him back up.

When he finds the slower pace, I use it for my speed change work within the lope. Again, I ride with a passive rein and with the horse in my hands with his face off the vertical.

Before you saddle up as you prepare your horse for riding, look at his body. Feel down his back and legs. Look for subtle changes in the muscle structures. While you are riding and schooling him, feel for the added strength and his developing ability to rebalance.

Introduction of the Canter

As the lope is developing and gets to this level, I introduce contact to the face of the horse and start the canter work. The lope is a three-beat gait with a moment of suspension without contact or frame influencing the horse. The canter is the same gait, but with contact and frame.

First stroke of the right lead lope departure.

Second stroke of the right lead lope.

Third stroke of the right lead lope.

First stroke of the left lead lope departure.

Second stroke of the left lead lope.

Third stroke of the left lead lope.

The Start of Transition Work

As this work begins to show improvement in movement of the gaits and the horse gains more strength throughout his body, I spend more time working on the canter. Every time a horse changes gait from a walk to a trot or from a trot to a canter or back down again, he has to re-balance his weight.

The value of transitions is in having the horse balance and re-balance with ease and grace. I begin by asking the horse to speed up the trot or slow it down. It's not difficult for the horse to re-balance to achieve what I'm asking. At the lope, it is a little more challenging because he has to deal with more momentum of weight in motion. For this reason, re-balancing within the lope usually takes a little more time to develop than during trot work.

Aligning the Structures

When I ask the horse to move from the trot into a canter, he makes adjustments in the alignment of his physical structures to accomplish the transition. He does this naturally when running free. When carrying a rider, he needs help to achieve a precise maneuver.

For instance, if I want him to transition from the trot to a right lead canter while traveling a straight line, I bend my lower left leg back to a point behind the horse's 14th and apply slight pressure. This leg signal asks the horse's hips to move slightly to the right. When I know his left hind leg is striking under the mass of his body, I'll lift the lower part of my leg up into the barrel of the horse. This is when I want him to take the canter depart.

With my hands, I want light contact with the face of the horse through the reins to the bosal. If I am on a straight line, the horse's head and neck should be straight on his body. As I prepare the hips so that he can get the correct lead when going to the right, he'll want to move his head slightly to the left of center. At this stage of his training, I let him. It's his most natural position to canter to the right.

A horse's body is designed to balance on diagonal pairs of legs and feet—left hind and right front or vice versa. That's called "diagonal balance."

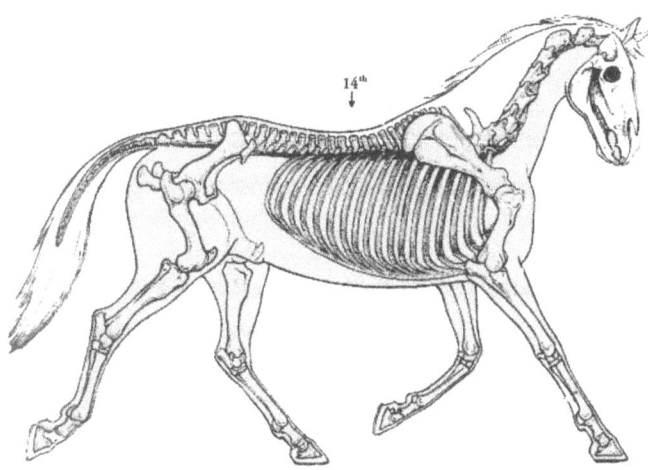

Horse moving forward on right diagonal balance.

Having the horse set up to make a particular maneuver, in this case to pick up the correct lead, is what I call "aligning the structures." The horse must actually shape himself, based on my signals to him, to achieve the movement correctly when carrying a rider.

Going to the left, everything is reversed from how it's described above with my body signals and the alignment of the horse's structures.

As the transitions become smoother and consistent, I start to add some influence with the right rein. I want to hold the horse's neck and head straight on his body through the transition from trot to canter, and while he is cantering on a straight line of travel. I want to develop both sides for moderate and slow speeds, up and down within the gait. Faster, then slower, then faster again, up and down in speed.

CANTER WORK ON A CIRCLE

My canter work on a circle should be easier if I have been using the circus pole to help develop "balance in arc" to teach the horse how to move with a slight bend, or arc, in his body.

When a horse is traveling straight naturally, he is on diagonal balance. That means an imaginary balance line in his body would be drawn from either hip to the opposite shoulder. When a horse travels in arc balance, the balance line would be drawn down the center of his body with a bend to it, and requires that more physical structures within the horse's body be in alignment.

Going to the left in arc balance, for instance, his hips would need to be slightly in toward the direction of travel. His ribs on the left side would need to feel closer together like one side of an accordion, and his neck and head would be bent in to match the arc of the circle.

When a horse is positioned or aligned like this, I don't need to prepare his hips for canter transition. They are already there! My left leg, on the inside of the bend, positioned at about the horse's 14th thoracic vertebra, causes him to yield his body to create the bend, or arc. My right leg, on the outside of his body and positioned slightly back just behind the 14th is what drives him forward. Because everything is in place, his body moves along the curve of the arc.

Developing "balance in arc," which is traveling while bent, is a learned behavior for the horse. He can do it but he will not maintain it. With bend in his body, he cannot close the spinous processes in his back and go to flight. This is why he continues to try to straighten himself to get back to diagonal balance so he can be prepared to go to flight.

Consequently, to make it easier for him, I do this beginning work in big circles. It allows the horse to maintain his balance while keeping his inside shoulder perpendicular to the ground. I don't want him to lean into the circle. He must remain upright.

A horse is able to canter smaller circles without correct balance simply by overloading his inside shoulder. But I don't want that. That's an evasion. That happens when his outside hind foot strikes the ground outside the plane of his body.

Remember, it's natural for the horse to travel on a diagonal balance. He wants to. He's programmed by nature to. When his hindquarters go off the arc line of a circle, he is out of balance. You must use your outside leg to keep his hindquarters tracking on the line of the circle, or, in other words, in arc.

If this evasion of his hindquarters—"leaking out" of the circle—gets into your training program, it will come back to haunt you when you ask your horse to work close to cattle with speed or when you need to turn him in a small area with speed. When you are ready, find the next distance from center, where he is struggling slightly, and work to develop more balance there.

SUPPLING AND STRENGTHENING EXERCISES

The three or four months of strength development work will not give me all the back and leg strength that my horse will need. To be able to balance and re-balance himself, while maintaining a high degree of carriage and frame, will take about three years of continuing work. But he should have enough strength now so that I can start to do some work to tax his joints to open and close while bearing more weight.

Most of the suppling and gymnastic exercises I use to develop my horse I learned as a boy and a young man. Most of the time, the old-timers used slang Western words to describe them. Up until I was exposed to some people in the eastern United States and Europe, I also used Western slang, which at times made it difficult for the people I was trying to help understand what I was saying.

I found that there was a universal language of words used to describe movements of horses that is used on both sides of the ocean. Some of my friends have taken the time to help me learn these words to describe the names of movements. It has certainly helped me in teaching, but I have not mastered it in my ongoing education.

RIDING A STRAIGHT LINE

Riding a straight line without a supporting barrier is harder than it sounds. When you ride down a fence line, it's not difficult to get the horse to move forward relatively straight. But when we take the horse into the open, he tends to wander left and right of center to the line of travel.

A lot of this is caused by a rider's weight in motion and the young horse's inability to hold balance through the shifting of weight. There is an old cavalry saying: "You need to ride your horse between your legs and your hands." That has a lot of value.

I will pick a time in my outside riding to work on straightness. Making contact with the face through the bosal, I'll hold the horse's head and neck straight on his body with my hands at home base. At the same time, I'll add a couple ounces of pressure to both legs, using my knees and calves on the barrel of the horse. I fix my eyes on my line of travel and stay very conscious that my pelvis is putting equal weight on both sides of the horse's spine.

My weight and motion need to move within the rhythm of the gait, centered over my pelvis; not forward, behind or left or right of my pelvis riding position.

As my horse moves forward, when I feel him start to wander from my line of travel, say to the left, I will add pressure to my left leg and close my right hand. The instant that deviation returns back to the line, I will soften my right hand, left knee and calf muscles back to the pressure I originally had.

When I first start straight line work, it takes a lot of corrections to hold a straight line of travel. The quicker I feel the deviation in his body and correct it, the better things will get.

I'll work on this little exercise until my horse can go a long way, two or three hundred yards, in a straight line. When that's established, I'll work on the same thing with a passive rein using the same leg influence.

The horse has to accept my signals without resistance mentally and learn how to make the adjustments in his muscle structures physically in order to hold the forward energy of his body between the parallel lines of my legs and hands.

Remember, his natural balance going straight forward is on the diagonal and his energy moves forward on those lines, right to left or left to right. We are not changing that. We are simply asking him to flatten out those lines in relation to his line of travel. He can do it physically, but it is a learned behavior.

THE LEG YIELD

A leg yield is an exercise that requires the horse to have some bend in his body from the poll of his head through his neck and ribs to the 14th of his back. While moving forward, he also has to move his inside hind leg and inside front leg (inside is on the same side of the horse as the bend in his body) diagonally across the plane of his body. This causes his line of forward motion to be diagonal.

Wall or track

This is a very easy movement for the horse to do because he is moving away from the slight bend in his body. It has a good suppling effect on his neck and ribs and creates activity in the horse's back that results in a slight openness of the spine.

Biomechanically, the leg yield requires the hind leg to move diagonally under his mid-body to support more of the horse's weight—or mass—over the hock joint when that leg makes contact with the ground. In time, this is something I need to develop to a high degree as I ask the horse to engage his hips farther under his body as his forequarters become lighter. This is especially true when working cattle and doing the tight turns that close cattle work will require.

With my horse going forward at the walk, I will ask him to come into my hands with his face off of vertical, which means not completely vertical. If I'm going to leg yield him to the right, I'll create some lateral flexion to the left. I do this by using my left hand to move the bosal's right bar against his jaw. At the same time, I apply some body pressure with my left leg ahead of the 14th for some contraction of the left oblique muscles for the rib flexion. This should cause him to bend, or arc, his body at his ribcage.

When that is established, I will move the lower part of my left leg—which I just used to create the bend, or flexion throughout his body—behind his 14th. I apply a slight amount of pressure until the horse's legs move under his mid-body in a forward stroke.

At this point, I still want my horse moving forward on a straight line of travel. When I am ready to change to the diagonal line of travel, I will move my right hand laterally in the direction I want his shoulder to move. If he needs more signal to understand, I can add in my left knee and left side of my pelvis. I want the right shoulder of the horse to strike off on my diagonal line of travel. As I initiate the hand and pelvis signals, I change where I look from straight ahead to the diagonal line of travel. In other words, I look where I want him to go. I want him to move onto this new line of travel without changing either the bend in his body or the contact with my hands.

If there is a test or brace from the horse, I reinforce my signals to the bosal or body or both. I want the horse to move forward with fluidness and with his front right leg and left hind leg moving on the same line of travel.

When I first start to teach this movement to my horse, I put a lot of lateral flexion on him but am careful not to over-flex him. Over-flexing is when the outside eye passes the inside point of the opposite shoulder. At that point I am putting the horse in the position where he can go to the opposite diagonal for balance. Giving him a lot of lateral flexion in the early stages of teaching this exercise makes the movement easier for him. The more he is bent, the less weight he has to bear over the engaged hind leg. Over-flexing him puts him back on diagonal balance, which he naturally would prefer. However, he would then learn to use that as an evasion.

Once he knows the leg yield at the walk, I start to work him at the trot. My rule of thumb is "teach at the walk, school at the trot" and always work toward quality of movement.

I want his trot to reach forward, not come as short choppy steps. As he gets better at the movement, I'll start to bring his head and neck closer to the center of his body but still maintain a flexed position. This helps achieve more gymnastic value from the exercise as it requires him to support more weight over the engaged hind leg.

A leg yield to the right. This is one of the easiest of the gymnastic exercises for the horse to do. I need to keep the horse going forward on a long shallow line of travel, and without getting too sideways. For a cowhorse I never want him to yield sideways from the cow or go sideways towards the cow. And I get all the side-pass work I need opening and closing gates.

In exercises where the horse is flexed or bent away from the direction of travel, such as a leg yield, shoulder-fore, and shoulder-in, the most gymnastic value is obtained with the minimum amount of lateral bend in his body. In these movements, the minimum amount of flexion or bend, while still allowing the horse to move in arc balance, is when his outside eye reaches the inside point of his shoulder on the same side as his eye.

As I move forward on my diagonal line, I want his front right and left hind leg to move equal distances diagonally in relation to his body. I need to feel that movement and make the necessary adjustments with my body and hand signals when there is deviation. If the horse's right shoulder is not reaching far enough, I'll add more to the left side of my pelvis. If I need to assert even more influence, I'll add more pressure from my left knee and then the right hand. If it's the horse's left hip that is not reaching far enough, I'll add more energy into the lower part of my left leg.

When I make these adjustments, I want to make sure the flexion in the horse does not change. He will try to bend deeper as you ask his legs to move equally on the diagonal line of travel. He would like to lighten the load you are asking him to support over the engaged hind leg to make the work easier. But the higher gymnastic value comes from him being bent just slightly off center of his body which puts more weight over the engaged hind leg and the front leg that is crossing the plane of his body.

At this stage of training, I want to develop this exercise so both left and right directions are good at the trot. Next, I want to be able to lengthen or shorten the trot within the exercise while riding on my diagonal line of travel.

I do not use the leg yield with very much sideways motion. I really want to keep it moving forward on a long, shallow diagonal line of travel. It is important that my cow horse not yield his shoulders away from the cow or to the cow when in a blocking position but he still needs to be bent to the cow. So I do my leg yield with a slight bend rather than straight. I try to stay away from exercises that create direct sideways movement. I get all the sidepass work I need opening and closing gates.

THE SHOULDER-FORE AND THE SHOULDER-IN

Shoulder-fore and shoulder-in are two exercises in which the horse's forward motion moves away from the slight bend in his body. They require the same configuration, or shape, of the horse's body as the leg yield; flexion of the head and neck, mid-body and one of the hind legs striking under the body mass.

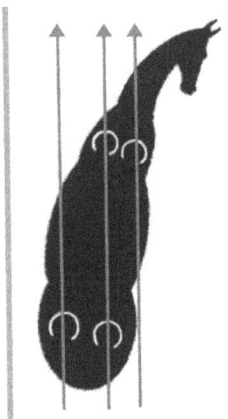
Shoulder-In

When asking for a shoulder-fore, I want the hind leg to strike the ground under the center of the body mass. When asking for a shoulder-in, the hind leg strikes the ground under the body mass in alignment with the diagonally-opposite front leg. If you were standing on the ground watching a horse come toward you and he was in shoulder-fore, you would see all four feet strike the ground. If he was performing a shoulder-in movement, you would see only three feet strike the ground. The engaged hind leg would be hidden behind the opposite front foot. A shoulder-in requires more balance and has more gymnastic value than the shoulder-fore.

In starting this work, I develop the shoulder-fore to a good trot before asking for shoulder-in. This exercise asks the horse to become supple from mid-body to his head. His hip moves under his body to support more weight over his hock joint on each stroke of that leg. It also requires him to be active in his back and move forward holding his shoulder on a straight line of travel.

Using a fence as a supporting barrier, I walk my horse forward with good life, asking him into my hands but not all the way to vertical. The contact should be good but soft (like holding feathers in the hands). I will ask for flexion of the head, neck and midbody using the same hand and leg signals as for the leg yield.

When that is established, I move my lower leg on the same side as the body flexion to ask the hip to move under and forward to the center of the horse's body. At the same time the leg moves, I will tighten my hand on the outside rein to hold the horse's shoulder on a straight line.

The outside shoulder is also used for my line-of-sight straight ahead of the horse. I want that outside leg to strike the ground on the same line of travel with each stride. If my horse's shoulders wander, I will make the corrections with my upper legs to help him hold the line and balance.

As soon as the movement is understood at the walk, I will move to the trot work and, in time, to lengthening and shortening the trot within the exercises. All of these suppling and gymnastic exercises have very little value at the walk but it's an easy gait to teach the movements.

It takes little effort for the horse to balance and re-balance at the walk but much more at the trot, canter and gallop. I use the exercise a lot and will take it up through the canter, using it with the shoulders away from the fence as well as toward the fence. When performed with the shoulder toward the fence it is called a shoulder-out.

THE CIRCUS POLE

I will continue the circus pole work to a point where my horse can hold arc in his body while maintaining softness in the fixed hands. The execution of transitions up and down in the gaits are well-understood by the horse. By now, I have gained some ground closer to the pole for my trot and canter work. My fixed-hand positions have moved to a high rein and a low rein and now should be slightly higher than when I first started the rein positions.

A right shoulder-in. This exercise creates good activity in the back muscles of the horse. This also teaches the horse how to balance over the stroke of the engaged hind leg.

I am now ready to start some work with the reins set to hold his head centered on his body. I arrange both reins in their high or low positions so the horse can make adjustments himself to create and hold arc in his body while moving forward on the circle.

Instead of cantering, trotting and walking close to the pole, and all in the same direction, I will work the canter out at the distance from the pole where he can canter with balance. Next, I'll move him in just to where he is struggling to hold balance to do some development work. After some effort on his part, I'll stop him by using my whip and body signals. I'll ask him to change directions by bringing his head toward the pole and by moving his shoulders with his outside front leg reaching forward and across the other front leg.

As he completes the turn, I'll let him out so he can canter with balance and I'll ask for the departure to the canter. I'll work the canter in this direction for speed and a slower canter with more collection. Then, I'll again bring him in where he is struggling and do some development work. When I am ready for the trot work, I will slow him down to the trot and bring him in to that distance, stop him, change directions and do my trot work like the canter. I'll then change direction for the trot work the other way.

Looking for a Good Effort

At the end of the trot work, I will bring him to the walk and then bring him in six or eight feet from the pole and really ask him to walk forward on that circle, keeping my body between him and the pole so he can't come closer to the pole. After seeing him make a good effort, I'll change directions on the same circle and repeat.

When both sides are worked, I will move back by his hip to get out of his way so he can get his loin area closer to the pole, and I will continue to drive him forward. By now he should be able to walk around the pole very close with his forequarters moving faster than his hips. After five or six turns, change directions and immediately asking for big effort.

I will use this same pattern until he understands the change of direction and can move through the turn with fluidness. I'm not looking for speed yet. When I start the canter work, I will put the horse where he is struggling slightly and do the development work for more balance. I'll let him out where he can canter with good balance and do my speed changes and maintaining gaits for a given amount of revolutions.

Changing Directions on the Pole

When I am ready to change direction, I will give him the stop signal. As soon as the horse stops, I immediately create energy toward the outside eye of the horse. As he starts the turn, I will bring my whip from down by the ground, up toward the shoulder to ask the shoulder to move with more speed. As the shoulder clears, I drive the hip forward, asking him to go right back up into the canter.

In my experience, most horses will need a few strides to get the canter depart when you get to this stage. Every once in a while you find a horse that is athletic enough to be able to re-balance at the end of the turn and get the canter depart on the first try. Most horses need a few sessions to develop the ability to re-balance.

The timing of your signals to move the shoulders through and immediately drive the hip forward is very important. To have the most positive influence, the energy from your whip needs to come from behind the hips but directed toward the hock joints. If the energy gets directed straight at the hip, he will move his hip outside the line of the circle's arc and strike off on the outside lead instead of the inside lead. I will work on this until my horse has the ability to execute a very fluid turn from the stop, re-balance himself at the end of the turn and continue forward at the canter with an inside lead.

Biomechanics of the Turn

To execute a correct turn, a horse has to keep his back open, top line muscle groups stretched, and hold his strength without being rigid. His face needs contact without any brace at the poll or jaw. The inside pivot leg, which becomes the departure leg at the end of the turn, needs to keep bearing weight slightly under the body mass through the turn and into the departure.

I want to take the time to get all these things well established before moving up to a rollback out of the stop back to the canter. My definition of a rollback is when I ask the horse to turn back 180 degrees from the stop before all the energy of the stop has left the body of the horse. It is a speed move that takes a lot of balance and re-balancing, along with strength. If I rush into the movement before I have good mental and mechanical understanding by the horse, I will invariably create bracing problems that will come back to haunt me when I put speed into my cow work. So I'll teach him to stop in arc, meaning with bend in his body on the line of the circle, to turn into the arc 180 degrees, and then depart at the canter.

These are three separate movements, each one to be executed at the completion of the previous one. When my horse is ready for the rollback, all my signals are going to exact more power. My body demeanor will be more powerful and everything is going to happen faster.

With my horse going forward on the circle at the canter, I will give him the blocking stop signal with my whip and my body. As he stops with his hindquarters engaged and his feet under his body, the energy of the stop moves through his body from his hips through his mid-body, up along his neck and out through the poll. As the last of the energy passes through the front of the horse, but before all of it has dissipated, I will increase my whip signal to the outside eye to start the turn. Next, I'll move the whip to the shoulder from his fetlock up through the shoulder blade; then drop the tip of the whip again to send energy toward the back of the hip, directed in the area of the hock joints to drive him through the turn and into the canter depart.

I will let him canter in that direction three or four rounds and then ask for another rollback. I don't ask for ultimate speed at this stage but faster than he was going during the three separate moves, one after the other. I want this to start to develop as one continuous movement. Big speed will come later.

THE SIDE PASS

Side pass work at the circus pole is easy to do. It's very helpful to the horse to develop understanding that he can move his front and hind legs across the plane of his body. For me, this little exercise makes my leg yield, shoulder-fore, shoulder-in and my hip work (*travers*) easier.

With my horse facing the pole, I set my reins in fixed-hand position with his head and neck straight on his body. I want his head right next to the pole. If I want to move him to the right, I will be on his left side looking down the left side of his body. I will create some energy with my whip alongside his body as he starts forward. I will block the forward motion with the rope that comes from his halter across the middle of the circus pole to my hand. This will cause him to step sideways with his left front leg and left rear leg stepping across the plane of his body to the right.

After each step, I send more energy toward the left shoulder and left hip. If he is reluctant to move, I will tap him lightly at the left stifle joint until I get some movement. I will keep asking for more movement until he has completed one revolution around the pole. Then I will give him a short 10-to-15 second break.

This is a good time to give him a horse pellet to get his tongue and jaw working so that he stays relaxed. The first time he is asked for a new movement, he can get a little tight.

After the short break, go the same direction again. I like to do this exercise three times on the same side and in the same direction with little breaks in between before changing to the other side. Later on, when there is good understanding, I will break up the pattern. One revolution to the right, then stop (no break time), then one revolution to the left, then right, and so on. At this stage, watch for the steps to be even, with good rhythm, and for the hips to stay on the same circle around the pole. It doesn't take very many sessions to get good fluid movement with very little energy from the signals.

When I am done with my circus pole work, I like to ride the same patterns that I have been working on for the trot, canter and side pass work. Doing the riding work on the same ground around the pole seems to help the horse try harder to re-balance now that my weight has been added to his back. I know I am going to lose some percentage of his ability to maintain balance and I will make adjustments for that.

Let's suppose he can canter at 22 feet from the pole in the groundwork. Now that my weight is added, at this stage of his training his ability to maintain balance might be 25 feet from the pole. The same thing applies for the trot work, but probably with less of a percentage loss in distance. The side pass work around the pole will be from a slightly different position. I will place the horse facing the pole with his face three-to-six inches from the pole and then ask the legs on one side to move across the plane of his body. For quite a while there will be less fluidness compared to the groundwork.

When I was buckarooing for a living, I didn't always have time for my circus pole work and to ride all in the same week. When I could, I would do it. But now that I have more time for that added work, I see it has more value than I use to think.

The Travers

Hip-in (or *travers* in French) is a suppling and gymnastic exercise in which you ask the horse to move his body forward into the direction it is arced. This helps my cow work and my pivot-foot turnaround. I need to have my leg yield, shoulder-in and side-pass around the pole well-established before starting this movement. I need the horse to be supple and at a stage where he allows me to move the structures in his body individually: legs, ribcage, neck and face.

Hip-In or Travers

If I am in too much of a rush to start this movement before I have good control of the mid-body, the horse will break behind the withers and not at the loin with no flexion in the ribcage and never achieve equal bend throughout his body. This means he is not bent around my inside leg. If this occurs, there is no gymnastic value to the exercise because the horse has lost his arc balance and returned to his diagonal balance.

Arc balance is a learned behavior and must be schooled in order for horse to sustain it. ***Travers*** is a movement that needs to be executed with the horse having equal bend throughout his body from the poll and neck through the mid-body and hips. That creates arc balance. Take the time to get good control of the mid-body with suppleness before you start.

In exercises where the horse is flexed or bent into the line of travel, such as travers (hip-in), renvers (hip-out), and half-pass, the most gymnastic value is obtained with the maximum amount of lateral bend in his body. In these exercises, the maximum amount of flexion or bend, while still allowing the horse to move in arc balance, is when his outside eye reaches the inside point of his inside shoulder.

When I am ready to teach this movement, I like to base it off a circle that starts and ends at a fence. If I am going to ask the horse for ***travers*** to the left down a fence line, I begin by starting a left circle at the fence. I want that circle to be big so that I don't require a lot of arc in the horse. The large circle gives me the time I need to get my horse bent on the arc and to get him thinking about holding that arc. When I get to the last part of the circle where the horse's head, neck and shoulder are trapped by the fence, I will ask him to hold the bend in his body and move down the fence line.

I will use the horse's inside shoulder (left shoulder) as my guide for his line of travel. I want his shoulder to remain on the same line with each stroke of his legs. The left hind foot will strike the ground slightly to the inside of that line, and the right hind foot will strike under the body mass. After three or four strides, I will soften the contact of the reins on his face to let him relax for 10 or so strides, and then do another circle to set it up again.

I need to build more and more strides in arc at the walk. When it is good, then I begin work at the trot; then at the canter. I'll spend six-to-eight months or longer getting this movement well-established. I'll use it a lot to develop my cow work, to teach the horse to hold the arc toward the cow when he is holding his ground on a lateral line, or when he needs to head a cow and turn back with it. I also use it for my pivot foot turnaround. That's where I want bend in his body so the turn will cover the smallest possible circumference.

A left travers or hip-in. I'm asking the horse to move in the same direction as the bend in the body, and to engage the hind leg from the outside towards the inside of the movement. This is a higher level of balance and rebalance for the horse than a shoulder-in. This movement also creates good activity in the back muscles of the horse and builds great strength over a period of time.

SIGNALS FOR THE HORSE

The signals I use to influence the horse start with the same ones needed to ride a round circle correctly. These include: a) contact with the face to create some openness at the withers; b) my inside leg calf muscle on the horse (ahead of the 14th) to create some contraction of the horse's oblique muscles; and c) my outside leg below the knee behind the horse's 14th to drive him forward.

By now, as I start the circle, I should be able to create most of the bend in my horse with influence from my inside leg and just a supporting inside rein and slight lengthening of the outside rein. As the horse comes straight before the start of the circle, the lower part of both my legs are behind his 14th, driving his hindquarters forward as the bend, or arc, happens, and, I hope, within one stride. My inside leg then drops forward to just below my knee and my outside leg stays where it is to drive most of his life forward.

A right travers or hip-in. This movement has more bend in the horse's body than the left travers. The more bend in this movement the more gymnastic value it has, as long as you do not over bend the horse. In this picture the horse is at maximum bend. The outside eye (left eye) of the horse is in alignment with the inside point of the right shoulder. The face is at vertical, creating maximum openness of the withers. This movement is being done at its highest value.

When I have the right amount of bend in my horse's body, I imagine driving 95 percent of the horse's energy forward from the hips with my outside leg (on the outside of the bend) and drive five percent of his energy with my inside leg which helps achieve his bend. It's not critical that I achieve those exact percentages. I'm sure it varies some. The idea is that I want the energy moving into the arc from the outside so that in time my horse can control and dominate cattle and have the ability to turn within a very small area with speed.

As my horse begins to bend, I make adjustments with my pelvis and upper body to match his bend and to ensure my weight is equal on both sides of his spine. As soon as he answers these signals, I soften them, like a feather, but don't remove them or abandon them. I want him to know he must hold that bend in his body. My softening of the signals is his reward for being obedient.

As we go forward on the circle, I make the little adjustments necessary to keep the arc in the horse as correct as possible. As I get to the end of the circle, and when his head arrives at the fence, I add a little to all of my signals except the "drive forward" signal, and move sideways and forward down the fence.

With my lower outside leg, I add more pressure behind his 14th to keep his hindquarters from drifting off the line of the circle and going to the fence. At the same time, I'll slightly squeeze my inside rein and move that rein to near the top of his scapula in order to hold his shoulder straight on the arc line of travel. Often I use a long stick or dressage whip that's about 50 inches long to enforce my leg on the outside. If I need to help him, I just tap, tap, tap behind the stifle joint. I don't hit him with it; I tap him.

In time, I want to be able to complete this movement without the support of the fence and hold a straight line of travel.

DEVELOPING FORWARD IN THE HORSE

"Forward" is not a specific movement but a term to describe the horse moving straight with energy in a specific direction with rein contact to the face and influence to different structures in his body. With flight being the horse's first line of defense when it perceives trouble, you would think getting good energy up in his body would be easy. In some it is.

But I have found and observed that a lot of horses tend to get a little dull in their forward energy when the rider starts to ask them to sustain openness in their backs through rein contact and, at the same time, move their body parts in different alignments to do movements.

THRUSTING LEG, LIFTING LEG

In his early development, I spend a lot of time driving the horse forward on a passive rein and forward with contact at the different gaits so that he learns the signals and that I can control the life in his body, bringing the energy up and down.

That is easy to do when he is on a thrusting leg; the same locomotion he needs for flight. When you ask a horse to sustain openness of his back through contact with your hands with softness, and drive the energy from his hips forward through his body, the base of the horse—the space where his feet strike the ground—becomes shorter, and the topline of the horse becomes longer.

In this case, the movement and biomechanics of the horse's legs change from pure thrust to thrust-and-lifting energy. Within that, there are many degrees, from a little lift to a lot of lifting energy. Each degree of this energy requires more engagement of the hindquarters, more tilt in the horse's pelvis, more contraction of the horse's abdominal and oblique muscles, more opening of the spinous processes in the horse's mid-back, and lengthening of the topline muscles and ligaments.

Obviously, it takes some time for the horse to develop the strength needed through his back and abdominal area to be able to maintain lifting energy for a long period of time, such as six-to-ten minutes of continuous work. If I always stay conscious that my horse is moving forward into a movement with good energy, it will take me three-to-four years to get a horse schooled to this level. However, I will never sacrifice the loss of forward energy to do a movement. If I start to lose life in the horse's body during a movement and I can't drive it back up to the level I think it should be while still holding the same form in his body, I will quit the movement and do some work to get the forward back in the horse.

Most of the time I drive him to a level higher than I was asking for within the movement. I then set him up to request the same movement or exercises. It is not hard to do but may require trot or canter work or both, with the horse in my hands. I will increase my influence to his back through my own back and pelvis, and put more energy into my signals than necessary. I need to use enough. As the energy, or forward, comes back up, I soften my signals and move in the rhythm of his gait, asking him again to maintain it.

To learn to bend well, a bridle horse needs to be very obedient to changes of speed. If I don't stay vigilant about developing his forward, I will never get the horse to his full potential.

DEVELOPING THE STOP

For my horse to be able to work cattle well, I need to develop a stop so that the horse can get his feet into the ground and stop quickly. This type of stop requires the horse to engage his hips under the body mass and break at the loin, keeping the mid-part of his back open and round.

Biomechanically, the stop should start from the hindquarters with the forward energy traveling through his body from rear to front. The last of this energy dissipates through the poll of the head.

At that point, I need the horse to maintain his balance over his hocks to be prepared for the next move. A stop that stays on top of the ground, like a sliding stop, does not have much value to me because in my work I need to hold and control cattle. In a worst-case scenario, that kind of stop might have me slide past the stock. The type of stop I use is easy to train because you ask the horse to seek weight that he was already balancing in motion and you make a dramatic change in that weight, down through his mid-body. I use my pelvis, back, legs and hands to signal the horse for the stop.

Signals for the Stop

I go through a mental checklist before I ask him to stop. Is my upper body centered over my pelvis with my back straight and my chest open or expanded? Are my reins short enough so I have the horse in my hands, toward the vertical or at the vertical, depending on how much openness I want at the withers? Are my lower legs still driving the horse forward? If these things are not in place, my stop signals to the horse will not get the best results.

Whatever set of signals you develop to ask your horse to stop, you need to be consistent to build the muscle memory in your body so this little check-out phase is automatic and subconscious.

When I am ready to initiate the stop signals, I rotate my pelvis (*ischium bones*) from my riding position to the back edge of my pelvis and sit down on my horse, letting my upper body weight fall through that part of my pelvis into the horse's back. I hold the thought in my mind about this position going all the way to the ground.

At the same time, as my weight goes down into the horse, I move my lower legs forward of the 14th and start to hug my horse's mid-body; upper leg first, then knee and calf, and at the end of the stop, my lower legs. This is done to help him hold the openness in his back as he re-balances over his hocks.

The slight hugging with my legs enforces the contraction of the horse's oblique and abdominal muscles. That, along with engagement of his hips, opens his mid-back.

While all this is going on, my hands move back and down only slightly as my pelvis changes from my riding position to the back edge of the ischium bones. I don't want to stop my horse with my hands. I want my hands to help him hold the frame ahead of the 14th to help keep the shoulders elevated so the withers stay open through the stop.

As the stop happens, I might need to make slight adjustments with my hands as to how heavy of a feather I am holding through the stop. If the horse's poll drops or lowers at the end of the stop, that means I'm applying too much pressure through the reins. If the poll pops up, I'm not applying enough. Finding that balance with my hands requires constant adjustment and keeps changing as the horse becomes more schooled. I want to ride my horses with only the weight of feathers in my hands for all signals; body signals as well. I go to wood or iron in rein pressure when necessary but return to feathers as soon as he responds.

Like everything else, the stop is easier to school at the walk and trot than at the canter. I will spend a lot of time building understanding of the signals at the walk and trot before I expect a well-committed stop at the lope or canter.

When my straight-line stops start to develop some quality to them at all gaits, I begin to stop the horse on a circle with bend or arc in his body. The signals are the same except that my leg on the outside of the bend in the horse stays in a driving position and the hugging with that leg is down to the mid-calf muscle only.

I want him to stop with good commitment of his loin and hips and hold the bend in his body. This will be a big help to me later when working cattle.

The Back-Up

I think of my horse going backward as forward motion in reverse. It needs to

Schooling the stop.

start from the hips. For the horse to back with fluidness, he has to have some openness in his back and lifting energy in his leg motion. The California-style bridle horse should be able to back a long way—as far as you would want him to—and with good speed. That comes in time.

Like the stop, I want the horse to back up by responding to my body signals. My hands act in a supporting role only. You should never try to drag your horse backward with your reins. Attempting to do that may cause him to raise his head and close or hollow his back, in turn causing him to drag his front feet. Also, dragging his front feet can be caused by over-engagement of the hind legs. That leaves him ill-prepared for the next maneuver, whether a turn or forward departure. In backing, my hands merely block forward motion at the start of the signals and hold enough face on the horse so his withers are open.

With the horse standing still with his back raised and his face toward the vertical, I close my lower legs around his barrel below the spring of his ribcage and squeeze until I get some motion. If that motion starts him moving forward, I close my hands to wood or iron. As soon as the motion in his body starts backward, I soften my hands and release the lower leg off his body, putting them back on without the squeeze for the next step back.

I repeat this until I get four or five steps. I then let him think about it for 30 seconds or so and ask again. The in-and-out rhythm of my legs can be either both of my legs together or one leg at a time. At the start, I exaggerate the movement of my legs on the release, coming straight out from his body and then letting my legs fall back to his body to ask for the next backward step. I keep asking for more steps with fluidness, not speed. I don't ask for speed for a couple of years. I need him to be able to flow backwards, picking his feet up and putting them down with fluidity in the motion for as long as I ask, whether it's 10 yards or 100 yards.

The most common mistake I see is a horse going backward while dragging his front feet. That means his back is closed, not open and round in appearance. If this gets into your training program, the horse will never back with fluidness or speed. To help correct this, I reach for the abdominal muscles with my heels or spurs to ask for more contraction. That will open the mid-back more. Sometimes a light tap at the elbow of the horse with the side of my foot or with a stick or whip will increase the energy enough for him to raise his back.

The more correct you are in maintaining your weight over the 14th, the easier it is for him to move. In not too long a time, the exaggeration in the leg signals will no longer be needed and the horse will back up with a slight leg movement from me and maintain good rhythm.

Speed to the Back-Up

When I think I'm ready to add some speed to the back-up, I start the horse backward and then change the position of my lower legs more toward his hips. How much life or energy I drive through my legs to his hindquarters will determine how fast we go backward. This increase in energy comes from my back by tightening my erector spinae muscles, and moving through my pelvis and down my legs. Remember, don't be in a hurry for speed. Take your time and really develop excellent fluidness and rhythm in the backup and the speed will be there.

Turn on the Forehand

This is an exercise I use for more control of the structures in the horse. Moving the hips in a circle around the front end of the horse does not have a lot of value to me in my cattle work. However, I believe this exercise is great for the horse mentally because it is very easy for him to do and requires only a slight re-balancing each time he moves his hips. This helps develop the horse's understanding that I can manipulate his body. In time, I will use that manipulation of his body to ask his structures to get into different alignments in order to do movements.

With the horse standing still, I make contact with the face through the reins to ask him to yield slightly toward the vertical. I want the horse to have some openness at the withers as I ask him to move his hips. If I was to ask the horse to move his left leg to the right under the mass of his body, I'd place my lower left leg behind the 14th with slight pressure until the hip moved. Just as the hips prepare to move, I soften the pressure in my leg and add a little more pressure into my right hand to keep the horse's right shoulder from moving. At the completion of the stroke of the left hind leg, I put the signals in again for the next hip movement. I repeat this until the horse has completed one full circle moving the hips around the forequarters to the right. I then reverse the signals to go in the other direction. Those signals are: right hand and calf muscle to create flexion of the face; right lower leg for the right hip to move to the left; and left hand to block the shoulder.

As the horse shows understanding of the signals and the movement, I work for more rhythm so that every step of the hind leg is the same. When this is achieved, I ask the horse to do the movement with more face toward the vertical so that his withers open more. I also ask the hind leg to reach farther.

At this level, I no longer ask the horse to do the movement with lateral flexion but rather hold his face straight on his body. This makes the exercise a little more difficult physically. Once my horse can do this exercise with an open back and good cadence, I will not school it very much, but come back only occasionally to check it out.

Turn on the Hips

This is an exercise I use for more control of the structures. This can be the first exercise for the horse to learn the mechanics of a turnaround and, in time, a turnaround with bend in his body looking into the direction of the turn. This is the type of turn I will need to be able to head cattle at high speed and be able to turn back with the cattle as they are turning.

I like to start this with the horse moving forward at the walk on a big circle, 60 feet in diameter. This requires only a slight bend in the horse to be on arc. I pick a place on the circle where the horse holds the bend in his body correctly. With my lower leg on the outside of the arc, I move my leg even farther toward his hip. This increases the driving energy to ask his outside hip to drive forward. If the horse maintains the bend, the increased energy coming from the outside hip will move his shoulders toward the inside of the circle, which is what I want.

At this stage, I look for only one step to the inside. I want that step to happen with the outside front leg of the horse reaching forward and across in front of the other front leg. As the outside front leg steps forward and across, the horse begins to move on a new line of travel. I will then release the bend in his body and transition up to the trot and follow that line for a short distance, about 60-to-100 feet. I'll then set up another circle and repeat it.

When the horse can move his shoulders sharply for that one step, I'll ask for two steps by not releasing the bend in his body while driving the outside hip forward. My signals to influence the horse are the same as riding a circle on arc. For instance, if I go to the right, my right hand and my right leg create the bend in the horse. My left hand controls the bend in the neck so that it doesn't change, and my left lower leg drives most of the life in the horse forward on the circle.

When I want the shoulders to move to the inside, I move my left lower leg back more toward his hip but without pressing into his body. From that position, I drive more energy through my body into my leg.

When my horse can give me four or five continuous steps with the outside front leg stepping forward and across in front of the inside front leg—with good energy but without speeding up—I am ready to start the work from the standstill. While I do this, I continue to build more steps from the forward motion of the horse until he can move his front end a full 360 degrees in equal steps around his hips.

With the horse standing still, I bring him into my hands. At the same time, I create some contraction to the oblique and abdominal muscles by using my calf muscles against his sides. I want some openness in his back. I then create some lateral bend in the horse in the direction I want his shoulders to move. The degree of bend I want is just off-center of his body. More bend will come later. Remember never to over-bend the neck. That would change the horse from arc balance back to the opposite diagonal balance.

Next, I reach for the hip with my lower leg on the outside bend of the horse and ask his hip to step forward. At the same time, I enforce my hand position and inside leg to hold the bend in his body. After one or two steps with the outside front leg coming forward and across the inside front leg, I let the horse out and ride forward with good life at the walk. I work on this until the horse can walk his front end around his hindquarters in a 360-degree circle.

I build it one step at a time to allow the horse to learn how to re-balance himself. I am not worried about speed at this stage, just good biomechanical movement with very even steps. I want this movement to come from the hip forward.

At this stage, it could be either the inside or outside hind foot that the horse pivots on as he learns to balance through the movement. In time, I want the pivot to end up on the inside hind foot because that is the type of turn I will need when turning cattle in a going-down-the-fence situation or other work outside that requires heading a cow.

At some point, after good cadence is established in the steps from the front end, I will drive forward at the trot and go straight ahead for 60-to-100 feet. This is the same as asking for this movement with forward motion already in the horse. I want to get this movement really well-established in the horse to a very high degree of quality. I continue to school it for a long time, asking for more improvement in re-balancing and increasing the length of the steps with the front legs until I reach his maximum potential for the way he is built.

The Turnaround

Biomechanically, the turnaround is the same movement as the turn on the hips except that I add direct influence to the shoulders to speed up the movement.

A complete 360-degree turnaround is pretty to watch if a horse executes it correctly. While it shows good athletic ability and balance, it has only occasional use in cattle work. The quarter-turn and half-turn parts of the turnaround have great value for my work and are used all the time. They need to be very fast and smooth. I use the full turnaround some of the time as a way to remind my horse to continue moving his shoulders into the turn until I ask him to stop. This re-enforcement comes about mostly when separating cattle, one class from another. It is especially useful when working your horse at a gate by letting some cattle go past you into another pen or alleyway while stopping the others.

A good separating gate horse is a sight to behold. But if you work big strings of cattle, hundreds of head at a time, the horse will get short with his shoulder movement. This is where a full turnaround, as the cows pass you going out the gate, will get him back into the right frame of mind. You might work your horse in the gate for two or three days before you need the full turnaround as a mental reminder to keep moving the shoulders.

The mechanics and sequence of the right turnaround with bend in the body and on the inside pivot foot.

SIGNALS FOR THE TURNAROUND

When I start the turnaround work, the signals I use are the same to speed up the shoulder movement when the horse has forward motion in his body. The same is true if I start the turnaround from the standstill. I set up the horse for the turn on the hips and, as the outside front leg makes the first crossover, I raise the outside rein upward and slightly back with a quick motion. The instant the shoulders accelerate, I release the rein back to the home base hand position at the completion of that step. I raise the rein again to accelerate the next step. As he completes that step, I let him out and move forward into the canter.

When two steps become quick, I ask for three, then four, each time asking for the acceleration with the outside rein while keeping my outside leg directed toward the hip. The key point to understand is that I want this turn to come from the hip forward so my horse can drive out of this turn with power.

> ### A Note from Frank Barnett on Turnaround Timing
>
> *"You need to pick up with the outside rein as the outside foot starts to leave the ground. If the horse has already made the first crossover, then Newton has taken over. The leg is on the way down to Mother Earth."*
>
> – Frank Barnett
>
> I certainly agree with this statement. However, on a younger horse, I will use the outside rein at a later moment as the first crossover is happening in order to get the turnaround started correctly. Then, I'll use the direct influence of the outside rein to speed up the next step.
>
> Once I am able to accelerate some steps, I will apply the timing that Frank is talking about, which is more correct for ultimate speed.

I want the turn to start on the inside pivot foot. He may switch to the outside foot if he needs to rebalance himself during the turnaround and then switch back to the inside pivot foot. As he gains more ability to maintain his balance through the turnaround, I will feel less switching from one hind foot to the other.

At the end of the turnaround, if he is on the outside hind foot and you need to drive forward out of the turn, like to go catch a cow, there will be a slight pause for a part of a second where you have lost your forward motion. If the horse finishes the turn on the inside pivot foot and the main drive is still coming from the outside hind leg, when you straighten the horse, your forward motion and energy is continuous. When the horse can accelerate each step for the full 360 degrees, I'm ready for the next level of signal influence.

Raising or "feathering" of the outside rein is a motion signal to the horse to move his shoulders. Feathering the rein is raising and lowering the rein next to the horse's neck. It may slightly touch the side of the neck or you may not need to touch the neck with the rein depending on the personality of the horse and/or his responsiveness at the moment.

You need to be careful that the rein doesn't cross the mane line of the neck. If this happens, the outside shoulder and leg will move closer to the inside shoulder, impeding the outside leg from moving forward and across the inside front leg. The outside front leg will stop next to the inside foot or behind the inside foot causing the horse to move more sideways than forward in his motion. This is a big negative because the horse loses his forward drive through the turn.

The motion of the rein moving is detected by the horse with his peripheral vision. The main function and design of a horse's eye is to detect motion. In natural light, the horse can detect motion 90 times faster than the human. He did not need to see the stripes on the tiger. He needed to see the tiger prepare itself to move. Horses are extremely sensitive in detecting motion and their survival instincts tell them to move away from motion, hence the spookiness we see in some horses.

Everything about his eyes is about survival, e.g., the ability to see separate images with either eye at the same time. The oblong pupil in the eye allows the use of more light than a round pupil which is better for focusing the sharpness of an image. So motion in signals from all parts of your body, when riding or from the ground, can have a positive or negative effect on the horse, depending on how they are executed. The horse responds to the motion he sees in the reins.

When the feathering signal is well-established, I start the shoulder acceleration with movement of the rein. I move my outside lower leg from a position back toward the hip forward to a more natural position at the 14th. I move my leg in and out from his mid body in a smooth rhythmic motion to ask the shoulders to keep up the speed. I don't ask for much speed at first but do want more later.

The outside rein is now back toward my home base hand position with a slight backward pressure to hold the inside hind leg on the ground as the pivot foot.

If my horse starts to lose some of his speed in the shoulders, I increase the movement of my outside leg. If he doesn't answer or respond to my leg, I add the rein back in for that step and continue asking with the leg.

If I have done my preliminary work well and with good understanding by the horse, this part should be easy. I take my time in building up the speed in the turnaround. First, I need complete understanding by the horse to maintain his shoulder acceleration from my outside leg, only using my outside rein to start the process. By now, my outside leg movement should be very slight to maintain speed. If I increase the rhythm and energy in my outside leg, his shoulder acceleration will increase. These horses can learn to turn around very fast if schooled correctly, but you need to be careful not to ask for ultimate speed when your horse has reached that level or you will burn him out. You can turn a horse around with moderate speed and with excellent correctness for his whole working life. He has only so many ultimate speed turns in his body. Save them for when the big money is up.

Moving Laterally

Moving laterally is very important in my cattle work. The horse is continually changing positions in relationship to the cow's body in his effort to control movement of the cow.

These changes in his line of travel, in order for him to get to the next position to hold a cow, need to happen very quickly and with balance. They may require my horse to be either straight in his body or bent through his body. They're often a combination of both within a few strides. Consequently, his ability to balance and re-balance during changes in line of travel needs to be developed to a very high degree and, in time, with great quickness.

Suppling and Gymnastic Exercises

To help my horse develop this ability, both physically and mentally, I use suppling and gymnastic exercises. A suppling exercise requires the horse to move forward or backward with bend in his body or part of his body. This type of work requires the horse to use more of the topline muscles in his body. But not in a rigid manner, more in an extended manner so that he can engage his hip or hips and place his hind legs more under the mass of his body to create some lifting energy with the stroke of his leg instead of pure thrust.

The gymnastic development comes about as the horse builds more strength and tone in these topline muscles when they are extended, giving him the ability to achieve and maintain his balance through the movement for longer periods of time.

I use these until the horse has developed a good understanding on straight lines of travel, work on a circle and then work on a diagonal line of travel. I do this work first at the walk, then at the trot and, in time, at the canter. In doing these gymnastic exercises, I will first do the work at the wall or some type of barrier that will help the horse hold a straight line of travel. This can make it easier for the horse mentally if he has some type of support on one side of his body. As he progresses in his ability to execute these different gymnastic exercises, I will move out into the open with no supporting barriers. Without the support, it is more challenging for the horse to maintain balance.

One of the first exercises I use is a slight deviation from a straight line of travel with the horse straight on his body. To do it, I ask him to move his shoulders about 10-to-20 degrees one way or the other. He will proceed on that line 10-to-20 strides and then I will ask him to move his shoulders back to the straight-ahead position, the same number of degrees, so that it takes the same amount of strides to get back to my original line. I then repeat this.

I will do three-to-five sequences before I give the horse a break. If I want the horse to offset his shoulders to the left, I ask with my left hand, the right front side of my pelvis and my right knee. This moves his shoulders to the left; to offset the shoulders to the right, the signals would just be reversed.

As my horse gets better with this movement from the straight line, and quicker to the signals without loss of cadence or length of stride, I move his shoulders farther until he can deviate to about 35 degrees from his line of travel. This requires him to handle rebalancing without loss of motion and, in time, to be able to accelerate the motion.

As the training goes on, I will ask the horse to make these deviations with fewer strides between transitions, left to right or right to left.

Shoulder-In to a Leg Yield

If I ride a shoulder-in with my horse flexed slightly to my right hand, I ask him to yield to the left by moving his shoulder off his line of travel. Holding the signals I have on the horse for the shoulder-in, I add in the same signals used in the previous exercise to move the shoulder to a new line of travel.

To ride a transition from a shoulder-in into a leg yield, the swinging motion of my horse's legs must change. As he makes the transition, his legs change from swinging straight ahead to swinging laterally underneath him and across the plane of his body. Biomechanically, a lot is taking place.

At the start of this movement the horse is going forward in right shoulder-in. The engagement of his right hind leg is forward and underneath the mass of his body. At the moment you change the horse to a left leg yield, the stride of the engaged right hind leg changes more sideways than forward. And the right front leg of the horse steps across the plane of the body to the left when you move the shoulder. They both should step equal distances. The movements of the legs in the leg yield become more of a scissoring motion. I want to get this good both right-to-left and left-to-right and, in time, from the shoulder-in to leg yield and back to shoulder-in.

Leg Yield to Leg Yield

Leg yield to leg yield is easy for the horse to do and gives me another chance to school re-balancing. If I leg yield in a given direction, I pick a spot to ride to. I then straighten the horse within three-to-five strides, flex the horse the opposite way and ask for the leg yield on that new diagonal line.

To make the re-balancing more challenging, I gradually shorten the number of strides between the transition of change from one direction to the other. In time, I make the flexion change in the horse from one side to the other with no pause at center.

Leg Yield to a Counter-Arc onto a Half Circle, Back to Leg Yield

This little combination exercise takes quite a bit of re-balancing for the horse. It also gives me a chance to work on the front leg on the inside of the bend, reaching forward and across the other front leg on an arc line. I ask him to execute the half-circle, which helps my turnaround work.

I start a leg yield forward on a diagonal line at the trot. When I'm at a spot that I want to do the half circle, I transition down to the walk and put a pause on the outside hind leg while still holding the other leg yield signals. I create this pause in the hind leg with a little backward motion in the same hand that is helping the horse hold flexion of his head and neck. That's the hand on the inside of the bend.

If I leg yield the horse to the left, the bend in his body would be slightly to the right. When I start him onto the half-circle, it's my right hand that executes the backward motion to pause the left hind leg of the horse.

As I feel him step on the start of the arc line, I pause the hind leg again just enough so that the front leg on the inside of the bend reaches farther than the hind leg on the inside of the bend. I want this half-circle to be quite large with the horse moving forward, using the pause or hesitation of the left hind leg to contain the shoulder on the arc line of travel.

When he has covered 180 degrees, I stop pausing the left hind leg and drive him forward into a left leg yield on a diagonal line of travel. In time, I will do the half-circle at the trot.

There is a lot of re-balancing going on in the horse through the half-circle. In addition, there is added value of moving the front end of the horse on the circle faster than his hips.

It is pretty easy, gymnastically, for the horse to move his shoulders away from the bend in his body. The balance he achieves is still diagonal through his body, as opposed to moving his shoulder into the bend of his body like an arc-turnaround.

In the arc-turnaround, the balance line in his body changes from diagonal (from hip to opposite shoulder) to arc-balance. That's where the balance line runs along the spine of the horse in the shape of an arc. Hence the term "arc-balance."

Quarter-Turns and Half-Turns

There's another exercise I use to help the horse mentally and physically as preparation for the part of my cattle work that requires the horse to hold a cow in front of him and not allow it get by him. I like to use a corral or arena for this work but it can be done outside as well.

With my horse in my hands, I start him forward from the center of one end of the corral and ride toward the other end. At some point, I will stop the horse and do a quarter-turn either to the right or left. Let us say I go to the right. As the horse finishes the quarter turn, I ask him to laterally flex to my left hand and left leg while he is going forward on this line to the right. I want only a slight flexion to the left, just off the center of his body.

When we get close to the fence, I ask him to continue to hold the flexion through the completion of the stop. I then ask him to make a half-turn to the left, into that flexion, moving his shoulder through and back to the same line of travel that we stopped on.

Three-quarters to seven-eighths of the way through the half-turn to the left, I change the flexion to the right. As his shoulders reach the original line, we move forward across the corral to the other fence, stop again while holding the right flexion.

Continuing the exercise going the other way, at the completion of the stop, I ask for a half-turn to the right moving the shoulders through and changing to the left flexion three-quarters or seven-eighths of the way through the half-turn, then back to the other fence and so on. I do this until I have done three, five or seven turns on each end. Then I stop in the center, do a quarter-turn and ride forward up the center of the corral and let my horse relax.

My body and hand positions are the same as my turnaround work and the stop. The main focus for me is to get the timing down for changing my leg and hand positions as I move through the half-turn so that I have the flexion changed in the horse by the time we are back to our original line of travel.

Chapter 5

INTRODUCING CATTLE WORK AND ROPING

Traditionally, the California-Style Bridle Horse's main purpose in life is to be able to handle and control cattle in all situations at whatever speed is required to get the job done.

Our first work in the starting of the horse helps prepare him to have some confidence in his rider, for exposure to the outside world with all the confinement to his body like saddle and cinches and hackamore and our body weight. Then the introduction to cattle starts and it is a long process, along with our suppling and gymnastic work, to finally reach the stage where the horseman can do it all in one hand with a bridle bit in the horse's mouth. It is like all the rest of the work; it takes time to get it done with balance and speed. So have patience and build it one step at a time.

Horses can get to really like to work cattle as they get to socially dominate another animal. A lot of horses show great interest early on in handling cattle. However, if it is developed incorrectly, they will learn to do the movements out of balance and with brace in their body. If this happens, the horse will not reach its full potential.

My horse's first exposure to cattle work comes when I feel I have enough rides on him to go outside and help make a gather. That varies from horse to horse, depending on their personality. The first few times we gather cattle and move them from one pasture to another, my main focus is to show my horse that he has the power or ability to move a cow.

Gathering a little bunch of yearlings at Bittercreek Ranch, Cleradon, TX, Crofoot Cattle Company

Mental Confidence and Understanding

A lot of times, all the movement around him and out in front of him can be disturbing mentally and emotionally for the young horse. I need to teach my horse that energy directed at the hip of the cow will send the cow forward. Energy directed at the mid-body of the cow will send it forward but veering slightly away from the pressure.

To stop or turn the cow, the position of the horse's eye needs to be at or slightly ahead of the cow's eye.

The horse has to understand that the influence to these areas of the cow's body happens correctly when his eye is looking at that area and his body is expressing energy. He also needs to learn to hold a position on the cow and not get closer to it while holding that position—whether standing still, moving or when we change position.

I want it absolutely understood by my horse that he doesn't go to the cow unless I send him there. He also has to learn to yield, or "give ground" to the cow, when the cow makes a run at him head on. This giving a little ground backwards is so the horse can reposition himself in front of the cow's eyes and make the block forcing the cow to go right or left before getting into the horse's blind spot.

Positions in Relations to the Cow

When my horse is parallel to the cow's body and holding a position on the cow, I want him to hold that line and not yield to the pressure from the cow. My horse is the wall and the cow must yield.

To begin this, I work to keep my horse in a position where the cattle are continually going away from him. Objects moving away from the horse are less threatening and can help build his confidence that he has power to make the cattle move. If an object or energy comes toward my horse from any angle, the horse's survival instinct is more apt to kick in so that he thinks he has to leave, especially during these first exposures to cattle.

So, when I first go gather cows on a young horse, I try to stay away from the area of the gather that will require him to make a lot of blocks or turn the cattle in a change of direction.

This is especially true if that block happens at the bottom of a canyon or draw where the cattle would be coming toward my horse from above. As the gather proceeds and the cattle start to bunch up, I'll be at the back of the herd, helping to drive them along.

I move my horse up toward the cattles' hips with enough energy to make the cattle move faster for a few steps. It doesn't take the horse long to figure out that his extra motion forward made the cattle go faster.

It is in the horse's nature to like to boss around other members of his herd of lower social standing. Because this is instinctive, he can, with his energy, make a cow move away. Horses tend to enjoy dominating cows. So I will move back and forth laterally across the rear end of the herd, stepping my horse off that line toward a cow's hip so he can drive it. When the cow moves forward with more speed, I will leg my horse back to the line and continue on across the rear of the herd to the outside edge.

I'll continue to change directions with my turn always being toward the cattle. At some point, I'll step directly toward a cow's hip until the cow moves faster, then leg my horse away. Exposing your horse to this a few times will begin to build his confidence that he has power to move a cow.

Some of the best cowhorses I ever made have been those that were the most afraid of cattle to start with. They naturally want to give ground or yield away from the cattle out of fear, especially when the cow comes toward them. This has to do with their sensitivity to motion in their eye, the speed of reacting to that motion and how innately brave they are, depending on their personality.

I will eventually use this desire to give ground to his advantage. He'll be able to use it to quickly change positions to block the cow when the cow is challenging him head on. But that will come later. Right now, I have him simply step up to move the cow away. As I see more confidence develop, I will expose him to more stimuli. This includes the sides of this moving herd of cattle, positions toward the front where cattle will come from behind him, and block positions where he meets the cattle head-on to change their direction of travel. There will be long periods of cruising along on a passive rein intermixed with short periods when I ask him into my hands and to step toward a cow to make it move faster or change direction.

RODEAR WORK

Rodear is a Spanish term for an open area where the cattle to be worked are held by a group of riders in a circle around them. It's used so the cows may be separated from one class to another or held for branding the unmarked calves.

The first few times I expose my young horse to this work, I keep him on the outside line to help to hold the herd in place. I let someone else separate cattle from the herd, pushing those cut cattle out through our holding line. This gets my horse exposed to cattle coming toward him. He has to react to them, either by stepping aside to let them pass by him or by stepping in front to block their passage through the line, sending them back to the herd if they're just trying to escape.

Not all areas of the line holding the herd will have the same amount of intensity. The shape of the ground and the surrounding area, the direction the cattle want to move, and the areas of the line the cowboys are sending the cut through all have an effect on where the most pressure is. The first few times we do this, I keep my young horse where the least amount of pressure is so that his movements to help get the job done do not need to be big or have a lot of speed to them.

If you are working a big string of cattle, there will be a lot of time to just sit in one spot very relaxed, moving occasionally to make a block. This teaches the horse that from a relaxed position he will have to move to do a little job and then he can go back to being relaxed.

When I think he is mentally ready and I can move his shoulders through at least a quarter turn, I'll take him into the herd to start separating a cow from the herd. I keep it as slow as possible for the horse. Waiting until we do a big string of cows that have been worked a lot is ideal. The cows will be gentler, more respectful, and they know what is going on and will quiet down shortly after the separating starts.

If the cattle have been handled correctly in the past, the older cows will be very easy to separate; you get position on them and drive them out of the herd and they leave.

Or, if they test you to get back into the herd, it will take only one or two blocks and the cow gives up. These are the cows I want to pick for my young horse. Eight, 10, 15 cuts and I'll give my horse a break and go back to the line to hold. In a while, I'll go back into the herd and do some more separating.

This is one of the jobs my horse, in time, needs to be able to do with such finesse that no cow can best him. To reach that level will take time and a lot of good cow work. Good cow work means my horse must learn how to position himself in relation to the cow's body to control the movements and direction of the cow. Because the horse operates entirely by memory, I need to be precise and consistent in how I position him to the cow and the configuration in his body. At times, he will need to be straight, then, a step or two later, hold bend in his body while always keeping his focus on the cow.

Marci Scott working one out of the herd. Her hands and right leg are in a good position to help the horse if need be.

These are a lot of basic things my horse has to learn right from the start or bad habits will form. So picking cattle that he can handle at this stage of training is very important to build mental understanding and emotional confidence.

Corral Work

Corral work inside is more intense than cow work outside. Everything is more confined and the corral limits the movement of the cattle. The positions we put on the cows with our horse because of this confinement express more energy, and things can happen quicker.

Generally, the horse has to move less distance to hold a position or to change a position before a fence also influences the cow. I use fences to my best advantage when I ask my horse to move his shoulders faster through the turns and maintain more openness in his back.

I like to start my horse on corral work in an alleyway 16-to-20 feet wide. I first work one of the gates down the alley where the cattle being sent will either go by my gate to another pen or be turned into my pen. This gives my horse more exposure to having cattle come toward his eyes with more intensity. If the cow is not meant for our pen, my horse has to stand in the gate and let it pass. The next one that is ours means he has to step out and block the alley so the cow turns and enters the pen.

The person sending the cattle down the alley might send two or three, one right after the other. Before they are all the way to my gate, they'll send another one that needs to go by. As the cattle go through the gate, my horse has to step in to block the gate so the last one goes by.

Another situation might be that I block the gate as cattle go by. The last one is for my pen. If this is the case, then the horse has to make that nice half turn to block the alley. Most of the time, moderate speed will get the job done. Some of the time, I have to move my horse fast with fluidness.

As soon as my horse shows good confidence in blocking the alley and my half turn is fluid with moderate speed, I'll move up to be the person sending the cattle down the alleyway. This person's job is to hold a group of cattle at one end of the alley. By blocking the alley or opening it up, I let one, two or more of the same class of cattle go by my horse. He will block the alley again until those cattle are on their way to the correct pen. Then we let the next one by.

All of this takes a lot of balanced movement from the horse. He has to send pressure—or energy—into the cattle so they'll want to go past him, and then immediately close the door. He'll have to move from one side of the alley to the other, which opens the door, and then move back again to close the door.

I want my horse to stay focused on the cattle in front of him. I'm really going to ride my horse with my legs for my turns to block the cattle, letting the energy from the fence stop my horse.

This is big exposure for my horse, with a lot of intensity and continuous movement. He's ready for it or I wouldn't be there. However, at this stage of his education, it is possible that I could stay too long for him. This requires judgment. I want to challenge him, get him to stay there for a while and do the work, but I want to be smart enough to quit before the pressure gets to him. The amount of time working cows varies from horse to horse. I will continue to build this work until he can stay in there and do several bunches of cattle without a break.

(Above) The horse is holding his ground and blocking position even though the calf is pressing him to get back into the herd.

(Left) This horse is in a very good parallel blocking position to keep the yearling out of the herd. Terry Crofoot is the rider.

Up to this Point

By now, he can cover 20 feet with quickness, keep his back open through the stop, re-balance and go back the other way while giving ground when he has to, and stepping in to apply pressure when it is necessary.

As my colt begins to improve at this work, but while still a long way from being finished, I will do some work in a bigger corral where I can send my horse 50-to-60 feet. I've found that in a relatively short period of time a lot of horses can get good moving laterally about 20 feet to block a cow if they get enough of this type of work. If I send them more than 100 feet, they can get lost mentally and lose some of their focus. This could cause them to learn to move purely on a thrusting leg with their back closed.

As I begin to go farther to block the cow while holding the line, the speed of the cow can build. That will require my horse to stop deeper and to turn quicker to hold his position on the cow. If my horse gets to the end of the line and is on a pure thrusting leg instead of a lifting leg, and I'm unable to open his back within one stride, he'll always be trying to catch up to the cow.

At this stage of his development, I can't open his back in just a few strides if he has built up big speed. I'll need to check him off the speed, get him re-balanced, and open his back so he can put some lifting energy into his thrusting leg. If I am caught in that situation, I will get stopped the best way I can and we will do our best to keep the cow from getting by us. If I have a job to do, I need to get it done the best way I can at that moment. But if I have time, I can school my horse while doing my work. If not, I will set up schooling time. It will help my horse if I build in gradual steps of 20 feet, 50 feet, 80 feet, 100 feet and then 150 plus feet.

In the lateral-line exercise, I hold flexion in the horse to help create arc balance. And I'll ask the horse to be more parallel to the cow to block her from getting by us.

There are times at the gate in the 20-foot alley when he would be parallel to the cow. But when he is the one cutting them off the bunch and sending them down the alley, his positions and movements are more diagonal in relation to the cattle.

INCORRECT RIDER BODY AND HAND POSITIONS

(Above left) My hands are too high. If your hands elevate, the horse's poll will raise with them. This makes it harder for the horse to get his nose in front of the cow.

(Above right) More direct rein influence than necessary. The horse is bent to the right but moving to the left with the cow. My outside/left leg is too far forward. The horse was moving with the cow on his own. I got in his way.

(Below) Good body position of the horse. However, my hands are higher than they should be. If my hands were lower, his nose would be lower, and reaching to get ahead of the cow's nose.

(Above) My left hand has moved too far across the mane line of the horse's neck. This causes the left shoulder of the horse to move more sideways than forward. The next stride he is going to be late with the cow.

CORRECT RIDER BODY AND HAND POSITION

(Top left) Good hand position and help. Also, good position of my inside leg.

(Top right) The horse has good position to the cow. The rider is helping with good hand position, and his body is in the center of the horse's body.

(Right) Good help by the rider, and he is not in the horse's way.

(Below right) Good body and hand help for this horse that is hooked onto a cow.

(Below) The horse and rider are very focused. Their position to the cow is excellent and the rider's position on the horse is also correct. This is the way it should be all the time. When it is wrong, most of the time the rider will do something wrong, and the horse ends up struggling with his balance.

BUILDING DISTANCE, IMPROVING MOVEMENTS

When the 50-foot distance gets good, we increase to 80 feet. Increasing the distance the horse has to move increases the difficulty of the exercise. Building this distance sequentially over time allows the depth of his understanding and the quality of his movements to steadily improve.

By the time he progresses to 80 feet with quality, he should be able to handle the task mentally and balance and re-balance physically with a fair amount of speed. When he can, then we increase to 100 feet.

In the normal course of our work, there are a lot of times to put this exercise to work in a corral. I will set up schooling sessions to work on it. There is great value in this work. When my horse has it developed to a level where he moves to the position to block and hold the cow on his own, the rest of my work to build this "cow-eating" bridle horse will be a lot easier.

In this sequence of pictures the horse is on time with the movement of the cow and maintains good position to keep the cow from getting back into the herd.

Chapter 5 — Introducing Cattle Work and Roping — Page 93

INTRODUCTION TO ROPING CATTLE

Roping cattle is another job my horse needs to master. He has to learn another set of positions relative to the cow's body that he must go to and hold until I move him to the next position. He has to learn how to stop weight on the end of the rope and re-balance himself as that weight jerks his body. He has to learn how to pull that weight forward. He also has to learn to hold tension on the rope when he is facing a cow no matter how the cow moves.

Horses need to separate in their minds the difference between the two jobs of working cattle. The two jobs are separating and roping. Up to now, I have been teaching this horse to move when the cow moves and to get to the cow's eye to stop or turn the cow.

When you rope a cow from behind, there is not a problem. However, as you move up and pass the cow, such as when you need to pull them or when you are holding a cow on the end of your rope out in front of you, a lot of horses will want to react when the cow moves. They'll move like they are separating cattle and tend forget about the rope.

For most horses, it doesn't take too long to begin to make the mental distinction between the two jobs. However, I have had quite a few horses in which this mental separation of the two jobs was a big deal and took a long time to get established. These horses were what the old-timers classed as real "cowie." Their strong desire to work the cow had to do with their sensitivity to motion in the horses' eyes.

With these types of horses, I will handle the schooling a little differently. If I rope a cow from behind, I make the stop on the cow directly behind the hip of the cow. It results in a bigger jerk on my horse, and I might have to slide a little rope around my horn if the cow has a lot of weight to deal with. But it will keep my horse's eye away from the side of the cow's body.

If I need to pull the cow, I will start the pull from the hip position, turning the cow around as I start the pull, and then adjusting my line of travel to where I need to go. It is much easier to start the pull going up the side of the cow's body toward its eye. Often, this is when this type of horse loses his focus about the roping job and wants to start working the cow. He may tend to look in toward the cow instead of straightening his body and maintaining diagonal balance while going away from the cow. The horse cannot pull weight unless he is on diagonal balance.

Branding with lots of ground crew help.
Mark Brum Cattle, Lockford, CA

AT THE BRANDING PEN

The branding pen is another place that can present a problem for this type of horse. It usually shows up after you have roped the calf and brought it to the fire for the ground crew to do their work of vaccinating, branding and castrating.

If my horse is holding the front feet of the calf, this puts him in the position of looking down the rope at the calf's head. When the cowboys' work is done and they let the calf get up to leave, it must go past my horse to get back to the cows. Sometimes my young horse wants to move to block the calf. Or the cowboys let another calf up to leave that's next to my calf and my horse will try to jump over to block that calf while still holding your calf. If they are turning the calf back into the branding pen and I'm on the heel end of the calf, I have the same problem.

To help these horses get over the confusion between jobs, as I come to the branding fire I will place my calf and horse on the outside edge of the area where the cowboys are doing the groundwork. In that spot, there won't be a lot of movement going back and forth in front of his eyes. If they are still working on my calf and let one of the others up to leave, I'll put leg pressure on my horse with my knee to hold his shoulders on the same side as the calf that is leaving. If necessary, I will make contact with his face.

If I am on the heel end, I will do the same thing if they are turning the calves back into the branding pen. My heading partner will know what I'm up against and will try to keep me out of trouble.

If these young horses are doing a lot of branding work, most will get it figured out in one season. I like to get as much of it fixed in the branding pen because the outside doctoring is more difficult to control if you are by yourself.

I have had some horses that have taken more than two years to get complete separation of the two jobs in their minds. It was worth the effort because each of these horses made outstanding cow working horses, the kind I was proud to show off and which ended up being good at their roping job as well.

My horses get exposed to the rope right from the colt starting process. That's when I rope their different body parts and swing the rope around them, throw it in front and to the side while they are standing still and I am on the ground. In the early riding outside, I will swing the rope and throw it all directions from their body. I'll also drag a log around so they can learn to pull. These are all simple things and not a big deal. As soon as my colts have some understanding that my legs can move them around, I go to the branding pen.

The first time, I'm going to rope only four to six calves, staying on the heel end of the calf if they are heading and heeling. If they are just heeling the calves and dragging them to the fire, I'll pick little calves so that the pulling weight will be less. If my horse is struggling as he pulls, I will slip some rope on my saddle horn so he can build up some momentum to keep pulling. I want to keep things slow and smooth. After a few calves, I will change to another horse. At each branding, I will rope a few more calves until he can stay for the whole set.

The branding pen is a controlled environment. If the cow boss is doing his job, it's very organized and smooth running. Everybody does his or her job, helps to set up calves for the other guy for the high percentage shots, stays out of the other roper's way, and makes sure a roped calf doesn't foul another roper's horse. This is a well-oiled machine, a great place for my young horse to start his roping job.

The outside roping can involve a lot more speed of movement and gait than in the branding pen. If I can't set up a sneak shot or I miss that shot and have to make a run at the cattle, things might get a little fast for my colt.

Laying a heifer down outside. She is being held by her front and back feet, and will be let up as soon as she is doctored. The horses are very relaxed. They know their job. Bill Berner on the front feet, the author on the hind feet.

I'll spend quite a bit of time teaching my horse to track cattle. Being a right-handed roper, I'll put him in a roping position slightly behind and off the left hip of the cow. We'll follow it wherever it goes and whichever way it turns until my horse learns to hold that position.

I like to wait until that time of year when there is going to be a lot of doctoring on young calves. They don't weigh very much and are pretty dumb about you setting up a sneak shot on them. Sometimes at the start, I'll tie my rope to the saddle horn and use my hobble strap as a neck rope up near the throatlatch of the horse so the rope stays down the side of his neck. Then, when I'm off my horse doctoring a calf, he will have to keep facing the calf.

Tying off to the saddle horn gives me the advantage of being able to use two hands to help guide my colt to follow and stop behind the calf after I have neck roped it. As soon as he figures out to keep tracking the calf regardless of which way it turns, and to keep facing down the rope, I'll go back to my long dally rope. It gives me more options with heavier cattle.

You can certainly do it all with a long rope dallying, but if you have a lot of calves to doctor, you spend a lot of time coiling up rope and it is more difficult to help the horse with both hands.

Tie-hard roping never was a part of the California Vaquero style of handling cattle, but dally roping was. The style developed in the discipline in Mexico and California. I'm a traditionalist, not a purist, and if I find something from another discipline that I think will help me make my style of horse easier, I'll use it.

In a year, my horse will be pretty good at his different roping jobs. In two more years, he should be able to handle everything I latch onto.

IN THE BRANDING PEN

Young Roy Bridges reaching for a calf.
Buckley Ranch, Winters, CA

Tim Welman on the head rope
and Roy Bridges reaching
over the hip for the heels.
Buckley Ranch, Winters, CA

Heeling a calf off the cows.

Dragging a calf to the fire. The horse is pulling nice and steady.

(Above) Roy Bridges getting down to doctor a calf

(Above right) Rygh Olson tailing one down and Jill Bridges slipping head rope so the yearling can fall.

(Right) Roy Bridges tying a bull calf down for cutting by himself.

Chapter 6
RIDING WITH THE SNAFFLE BIT

MY EARLY EXPERIENCES

In the 1940s and 1950s, when I was a boy and a young man, my exposure to the California Vaquero style discipline occurred in southern California, specifically the San Joaquin Valley. Horses weren't started until they were four-to-six years old because they needed to be strong enough to do a day's work. There was no trailering of horses on ranches in those days. You rode to your work, did the work, then rode back.

Horses were started in the big hackamore, put through the weight-changing process of the hackamore discipline, into the two-rein, and then into the bridle, never having a snaffle bit in their mouths. Where I was raised, the people I was around did a lot of groundwork before starting the riding part. A lot of that groundwork was driving the horse in a 36-foot square pen with a driving caveson on his face, no bit. At that stage of my life, I thought snaffle and bar bits were for work horses and driving horses.

In 1955, I left California and went to Nevada to buckaroo and for the first time saw a horse being ridden with a snaffle bit. I didn't know what to make of it. I had driven a lot of work horses and a couple of light-weight driving horses and I knew they didn't feel like the hackamore horses or old bridle horses I was given to ride back home. So I thought that riding a horse in the snaffle bit could not be very good. And I didn't want to try. I rode my string of horses in the hackamore or bridle, depending on what they were. I was so much a product of the environment I was raised in, and, along with youthful stubbornness, that I could not see any good in it.

The horses on that first outfit were not very good so that didn't help. I saw a couple of horses in the snaffle that were pretty handy at the next outfit I worked for but most of the horses I saw weren't very good there, either. After about a year and a few outfits later, I went to work where the horses were, on average, good to well-broke. The cow boss and the buckaroos were fussy about their horses, and I saw some really nice horses being ridden in the snaffle bit. Then I wanted to try it and they helped me by lending me a snaffle set-up to use on my string of horses. I also asked a lot of questions. I'm sure they thought the questions were dumb, but they answered them, or at least tried to. I was the youngest in the crew by quite a bit.

Throughout my career in the cattle business, the people I've had the privilege to work with, for the most part, have taken great pains to help me get better and understand more.

I rode every horse in my string in that snaffle, trying to get a feel for it. These were nice horses, pretty well-broke, so that sure helped. I thought I would have to use my hands differently than with the hackamore but one of the older men told me to do the same as with the hackamore, just leave out the little bumps and pulls used to add to the nose button and bar signals.

Tips from Experienced Hands

After I started to ride with it, I would watch one of the other guys as he asked things of his horse. He would show that when the hand signal was above the mane of the horse, the snaffle lifted higher into the curve groove of the lip and got the best response. I noticed with my horses that they didn't all feel the same in my hands. They answered the signals and moved well, but some gave more feel back into my hands.

It was quite a few years later before someone explained to me about the thickness of the soft tissue at the curve groove of the lip. When you feel the curve groove of the lip from inside to the outside, it has a tapered feeling to it. The thinner it is, the quicker and more responsive the horse will be to the effect of the snaffle lifting upward in the mouth.

The main principle of the snaffle is to create a lifting effect. The speed of this lifting effect is directly related to the thickness of the curve groove. The thicker it is, the less feeling you will get back to your hands, and the slower the horse will respond to the snaffle signal. This is something that you certainly can work around. It has more to do with the lightness you feel in your hands at this stage of training. Later in the process when you start to put the horse in the bridle bit, the curve groove will have very little or no effect because a bridle bit works off the surface of the tongue and the hard palate of the mouth. The spade bit, or any other bridle bit that has brace bars, can create a slight feeling effect in the curve groove if the bit is placed properly.

A text book fence turn by a very nice snaffle bit horse. Mike Bridges and Smokey at the 1987 Snaffle Bit Futurity.

Using the Snaffle Today

You can make a real nice horse just using the snaffle bit, and they can become very light in it. I have made a few bridle horses just using the snaffle bit, then going to the two rein and into the bridle, and they were nice horses. However, I have found that going by through the hackamore process of changing the weights with the ropes and different size bosals, I can lighten the front end of the horse quicker. That's important in the movements my horse needs to do in my cow work.

Also, with the hackamore my horse will get to a point where he will work inside the hackamore on his own when I drive his hip forward and I'm holding a supporting rein to the bosal. He opens his back without me having to bring him back into my hands. With the snaffle bit, if I don't bring him into my hands as I'm driving the hip forward, he will just go faster in the gait and won't change the topline of his frame by opening his back. This is because he supports the snaffle with his tongue and hard palate. It takes activation of the reins to change the feel for response.

The hackamore is fluid on the face, always containing some movement from the energy of the gait the horse is in or the hand signals you give.

I ride all my horses in the snaffle, from a little to a lot depending on the curve groove of the lip and what I'm going to do. If I know I'll be doing a lot of long trotting on a certain day to cover country, I will probably use the snaffle because I won't have to support it as he trots and I can hold a long passive rein.

In the hackamore, I do need to support it enough so that it doesn't bounce on his nose. If I know I am going to rope a lot of cattle and my horse is still in the 3/4-inch bosal and one of the 3/4-inch ropes, I would probably put on the snaffle because my snaffle reins are only 1/2-inch yacht rope and I have small hands.

Over the years, my training program has evolved to where I do my groundwork using the snaffle bit. Most of my early and intermediate riding is in the hackamore. Yet if I get a horse that has tissue paper thin curve grooves, I am going to make a snaffle bit horse out of him with very little or no riding in the hackamore. The finishing stage for either type of horse will be the two-rein process into the bridle bit.

The California Vaquero Bridle Horse discipline is more than 480 years old and has evolved from a war horse to a cow horse. The introduction of the snaffle bit to the discipline is relatively new, probably entering within the last 70 years, and I think it is a great addition to the equipment we use to develop this type of horse. It has given us more avenues to explore.

Cavaletti work is very good to help the horse learn how to get his feet off the ground and rebalance himself. Teaching this from the ground before riding gives the horse the chance to find the balance while only dealing with his own weight. Gilbert Guerrero, Matador Ranch, Matador, TX is doing the groundwork and riding.

MORE SNAFFLE BIT

A young horse going over Cavaletti in an arc. Ridden by Roy Bridges. This can help the horse learn to get his feet off the ground, while maintaining the bend in his body. This is a different balance than doing Cavaletti in a straight line.

Starting a right turn-around on a green colt. Ridden by Roy Bridges.

Chapter 7
INTERMEDIATE HACKAMORE WORK

DEVELOPING SELF-CARRIAGE

Up to now, I have gone through three rope changes in the 3/4 inch bosal and have changed to the smaller 5/8-inch bosal. The first rope for this bosal weighs about 2 pounds-to-$2^{1/8}$ pounds.

I'm also starting to get some instances of self-carriage from my horse. That doesn't happen every time I drive him forward. But when things are right, our mental connection is good and he is in balance. He frames himself by bringing his face toward the vertical, and opening the withers and his mid-back.

It is a neat feeling when it first starts to happen. You know that your horse has reached a new level. The trust between each of you is now at a point where he allows you to manipulate the structures in his body without bracing. If he does happen to put a brace in, it is so slight that when you address the brace he releases it. His testing of you and your program occurs less often, with less intensity and for a shorter duration.

Getting to this point takes two-to-three years of work, with most horses arriving at this point closer to the third year. If you buckaroo for a living, you have a string of horses you are riding and developing. How many may depend on the country you are riding.

RIDING MY STRING

I like to ride a string of five horses that are in different stages of development. I'll also have a broke bridle horse as my sixth horse for a backup. Most days, I'll ride one horse all day for six-to-sixteen hours. That means, obviously, I spend a lot of time with them. My schooling work is spread throughout the day as I do my work.

Often, my day consists of short periods of intensity and long periods of just cruising along. I often will take along one of the younger, greener horses in my string with a horse that I could get my day's work done on. I would have the colt saddled and put a snaffle bit in his mouth with the reins done up so he couldn't get his nose lower than his knees, preventing him from trying to graze.

What is Self-Carriage?

Self-carriage is described by different people in different ways. When I refer to self-carriage in a horse, I'm referring to a change in the frame of the horse that is created by the horse himself without having him in my hands.

I am riding the horse with only a supporting rein influence to the bosal. This supporting rein position keeps the hackamore from bouncing on the face.

I ask the horse to drive more forward from the hips by influence from my legs behind the 14th. And as I ask for this increased drive, the horse changes the position of his neck, poll and face to open his withers on his own. He creates a longer topline and a shorter base. To me, this is self-carriage. The horse is creating his own frame.

If I rode him in the hackamore, I would tie it behind the saddle so he couldn't chew on my hair rope. I use the snaffle instead of the hackamore because when he lopes on his own, the bosal bounces on his nose. That's something I don't want because the horse will start to push his nose out and up in his attempt to support it. Raising his head causes a softening of the nuchal ligament in the neck and a closing of the withers. This is just the opposite of what I am trying to develop.

In my buckaroo days, when I got about a half-mile or a mile from camp, I would turn the colt loose and let him follow me as I went about my work. At times, these colts would go off and explore things or take a different trail and get themselves into a little trouble. After a few minutes, they would come running back, whinnying their heads off.

For a while afterward, they would stick to you like a postage stamp. It worked real well in helping the horse get over things that might bother him outside with the confinement to his body of the saddle and the snaffle bit. I would pick a few times during the day to ride the colt and to get a little work done without overriding him.

In a year of buckarooing, I would average about 80 days of riding on each of the five horses in my string by packing one or two of the greener horses with me when I left camp. That is not a lot of rides per horse per year but it is quite a few hours spent with each horse with motion in their bodies.

For the last 15 years, I've been going down the road conducting clinics and traveling with just two horses at a time. That means I make more rides per horse per year than when I was buckarooing. Still, I ride fewer hours with motion in the horse per ride. However, this does mean more minutes of intensity in the schooling work in the clinic environment. Despite this, I find that it still takes about the same timeframe, around three years, to reach the point where the horse starts to work inside the hackamore on his own.

I've come to the conclusion that whichever way you train your horses, you have to do enough good work for long enough for the horse to develop the strength in his back and the rest of his body to be able to maintain an open back and rounded topline before he will seek self-carriage on his own.

By now, along with the moments of self-carriage, my horse's response to my hand and body signals has developed to the point that he will come into my hands almost every time with just the closing of my fingers. I don't have to put in the little bumps to enforce the nose button unless there is a slight brace. When he is in my hands, the weight of the feather has become even lighter. All of the movements I ask of him now have good balance and can be done with moderate-to-good speed.

Challenging Your Horse

I continue to challenge him to become faster to my hands. The bars of the bosal are now closer to his face but still not tight. How close depends on the individual horse. I keep pushing him to answer my signals with more speed within his ability to re-balance himself. If I ask him to answer a signal faster than he is able to re-balance, he will brace. If I ask him to answer too fast with bend in his body, he will try to push his head and neck to the counter side to get back onto diagonal balance.

One quality leads to the other; more ability to balance and re-balance, then more ability to answer a faster signal.

I am going to make two more rope changes in the 5/8-inch bosal. These changes usually will come a little faster than the development work in the 3/4-inch bosal. When he gets to a point where I feel he is as fast or faster to the signals, I will move down to the next lighter rope, dropping about a quarter-to-a-half pound of weight.

My horse is getting handy now. He knows his job and can really move his body around. He is getting to be a lot of fun to ride. It is easy to become a little greedy asking for more from him at this stage of his development and wanting more speed in the movements than the horse can handle. Be careful to build it one step at a time to develop more balance in the horse.

HIGHER LEVELS OF BALANCE

At this stage, I school my horse with his face more toward the vertical and push his hips more forward under his body. I will ask for more openness in the back and much more roundness in the topline, whether he is straight on his body or has bend in his body.

When I ride him, I canter much smaller circles with lots of changes in speed up and down. I also ride a circle and make a change of lead with a slight slowing within the gait to a circle in the other direction. Now I ask for that change within one or two strides. By now, I've also started to canter the easier counter-bend exercises.

On the straight-line canter, I've begun lots of speed-change work with changes of direction to left and right diagonal lines of travel. I lope and canter him more on uneven ground outside to challenge him to re-balance himself.

In the turnaround, I start to ask him to turn one way, stop, and immediately turn back the other way with a little more speed. I also start to ask for a little more bend in his body at times.

In the back-up, I want more distance and more cadence of steps. I now want a lot of work to refine the forward-to-the-back-up until he can balance himself over his hocks at the end of the back-up.

The circus pole work has continued but is now closer to the pole. I can now ask him to work with more openness in his back and his face at the vertical. I will challenge him to canter closer and closer to the pole with his shoulder perpendicular to the ground and move faster through the rollbacks.

By now, his transitions up and down between trot and canter are very correct and smooth on the pole. In side-passing him around the pole, his hips can scribe a nice round circle. Strength throughout his body has substantially increased. I will continue to ask him to sustain each part of this work for longer periods of time.

I never work him to fatigue but ask for effort on his part. If I have time, I will ride the same work at the pole as soon as I'm done working him from the ground.

The circus pole is a continuing part of my horse's development. Even when he is a straight up bridle horse, I will still use it at times to tune him up.

THE POST PEN

There is a place to go in groundwork beyond the circus pole to develop an even higher degree of balance and ability to rebalance. This is the "post pen," as my friend Frank Barnett of Williston, Florida, refers to it. I often call it the "square pen."

> **Post Pen Historical Notes from Frank Barnett**
>
> Working a horse around a single pillar goes back to Pluvinel's time. He was Louis XIII's horse trainer (see Le Maneige Royal). It took the contemporary genius of legendary California horseman Harold Farren to enclose the single pillar with a square. Everything I know about the post pen was taught to me by Harold Farren.
>
> According to Pluvinel, working a horse around a single pillar brings out the balance, gentleness, lightness, resources and vigor and gives those everlasting qualities to those not naturally endowed with them.
>
> Harold Farren: "The post pen eliminates eight months of hard work." Also "helps clean their minds up."
>
> Frank Barnett: "There are no shortcuts in training the horse. But there are ways to make your progressions go faster. The post pen is one of them."

When I met Frank, I had been using the circus pole for about 30 years and didn't know there was a step beyond the circus pole to help the horse develop more balance. Frank introduced me to the post pen. Now, it's become part of my training program. It has great value when your horse gets to this level.

The post pen is 22-to-24 feet square with a fence that is about 40 inches high, 12 inches wide at the top, and open underneath so that the horse does not bump his knees when he is up against the fence with his head to the outside. A circus pole or post inside it is set two feet off center. The fence can be made portable and set up around your circus pole.

The small size of the pen creates a lot of intensity and energy for the horse. My positions, relative to the horse's body to drive, turn or block him, are the same as when I use the circus pole but I need to be much more precise. Every mistake gets a big reaction from the horse.

I believe the post pen's intensity level is eight times higher than the circus pole, but the higher rewards are there if it is used correctly.

When I first take a horse into the post pen, I will "pattern" him. The rope that I use at the circus pole can be used here also. It's attached to the horse in the same manner, usually at the stub of the halter inside the chinstrap of the snaffle. But I am not going to attach the rope to the post or the circus pole in the pen. I will maintain it in my hand along with my driving whip. When I do changes of direction, I will drag the middle of the rope against the circus pole in the pen to help create the hand effect to the face.

This patterning process will have less intensity than an actual work session in the post pen later on. I'll simply just trot him and do some change of direction work on the wide side of the pen. He'll already know how to go around, and I want him to be able to canter within a 20-foot diameter. The first couple of times in the pen, I want him to get used to the increase in energy that the pen creates. After some good trot work, I will walk him into a corner and ask him to stand upright to the side of the fence with his head and neck on the outside of the fence.

After he stands for a brief time, I will guide and drive him out of that corner and over into the next corner. I want him to become comfortable but stand on all four feet. I will move him to the next corner and continue to repeat this until I have put him into each corner at least five times. I want the horse to learn that each corner is a sanctuary; a place to rest from the intensity of the work but not a place to go to sleep.

The next day in the post pen, I will continue with the patterning work. I will increase the time he spends trotting and ask him to canter some. I want him to work a little harder than on the first day to increase his respiration. The fixed-hand positions will be set somewhere between the point of his shoulders and the top of his scapulas with his face just off of the vertical. Of course, this depends on each individual horse. The circus pole work will determine where this horse is in his development. In the post pen, I use the same fixed-hand positions that I use at the circus pole.

While I probably work him at the vertical in the face on the circus pole to ask for the withers to be completely open and the mid-back to be open from the drive of the hips, I will let him off the vertical in the post pen in order to make re-balancing easier in this confined area.

When I feel I've done enough trot work, I allow him to walk and point him at one of the corners, block his side, drive his hip and send him into the corner. Here I let him relax, but standing up straight. If necessary, I touch his inside hind leg with my whip until he stands on it slightly ahead of the other hind leg.

When I am ready to have him leave that corner, I put a little pull on the rope that goes to his halter. I drive his hip forward with slight motion from the whip, block his side with my body and send him to the next corner. There I ask him to be straight into the corner and stand on the inside pivot foot.

After four or five corners, I approach him while he's standing in the corner and scratch him a little bit. Sometimes I sit on the rail up by his head. I keep my body relaxed. If he tries to move backward or sideways to leave, I correct him. He has to stay in the corner. After this little break, we do more corners until he has gone to each corner four or five times. When I am ready to stop the work, I'll drive him into a corner where I unrig him.

The next time we work in the post pen, we'll do more canter work and changes of direction. By then, he will probably begin to look into the corners as he trots or canters around on the circle. I look for this. I pick a time to bring him down to the trot and change direction to send him into a corner. I let him stand 10-to-15 seconds on the inside pivot foot, and then send him to the next corner with good life and drive.

Once he understands the concept of the work, that is, going into the sanctuaries when I send him there, I break up the pattern. I let him stand, then send him out of that corner and back onto the circle to trot or canter for a few rounds, change his direction, send him into a corner, have him stand, then send him back onto the circle or to another corner, or do all of the corners. At this stage, when I send him to a corner it is the one in front of him that he is looking at.

CIRCLING THE POLE IN THE POST PEN

Coming out of a corner. Developing the driving power of the left or right hind leg helps the horse develop explosive power from a standstill into a movement.

When he is on the circle, he is going through the corners deep enough so that he has to re-balance at each corner. In 12 feet or less, he has to re-balance for the next corner. When I take him off the circle and send him into a corner, he must re-balance for the stop.

If I am consistent about the pivot foot, he will start to stop with his loin committed and his hips underneath him. In that case, his pivot foot is the deepest leg in the stop. This puts him into a position to come out of the corner over his inside hind leg when I put the little signal on the rope and drive the hip forward. This is the kind of drive and turn I want for my cow work.

When all of this starts to become good, I begin to send the horse from the corner he is standing in to one that is directly behind him. This requires him to move his shoulders through and do a complete half-turn. When I'm ready to begin this work, I will slow things down to the walk until he develops understanding.

By now, when I put the signal on the rope to bring his head toward the direction I want him to move, he is driving from the hips forward on his own or with very little signal from the whip. As he starts out of the corner, I will reach across in front of him with my stick or whip to block his outside eye and to create a little motion. This causes him to move his shoulders through. As he comes through, I move with him and send him into the corner. I repeat this until I have done five or so transitions from corner to corner.

I'll do this toward the end of each session until the horse has good understanding and he can trot between the corners. Then I will add this exercise to the program.

As the work progresses, its speed and intensity increases over a period of months. Most of the work will be at the canter on the circles and through the change of directions, and back to the canter. It would look like this: into the corners at the canter, at the end of the stop coming out of the corner at the canter, I send him to the next corner or back onto the circle or roll him back to the corner behind him or to a diagonal corner.

You can do all kinds of combinations coming out of the corners with the horse. Going to the corner in front of him or the one directly behind his hip which will require the horse to complete a half-turn, or you can send him across the pen to a corner that is diagonal to the corner that he is leaving.

The speed he achieves going to the next corner depends on how hard you drive the hip.

At this stage of development, the work in the post pen is all trot and canter. In time, you want him to be able to make changes of direction or come out of a corner in the canter gait. The post pen is a place of intense work for short periods of time, 10-to-20 minutes, once or twice a week.

After I get past the patterning stage, I have found that as my horse gets better in the post pen, his ability to make combination moves on cattle dramatically increases. Frank Barnett is a master of the post pen as well as many other disciplines. He gets great work done refining higher levels of balance. With Frank's help and the hours spent in the pen, I can see great value in its use to help develop my type of horse.

(Top and Above) Dusty making a turn back to the left to go right around the square pen. He is well balanced over his hocks and using a lot of power in the turn.

(Right) A turn back to the right with horse on his inside pivot foot (right hind). The first push into the turn will happen from the left hind leg. The second push forward will happen from the right hind leg, which was the pivot foot. This is a well balanced turn with lots of power.

Square Pen, cont.

This sequence of photos gives you a good look at the horse preparing himself to stop and then the actual stop with the hip engaged. The square pen is a great place to bring your cow horse stop up to new levels of performance.

Here the horse is cantering around me between the corner of the pen and the post in the middle. This is the short side of the pen. There is ten feet between the corner post and the post. As my horse advances in his training, I keep challenging him to do more, relative to his ability to rebalance in less strides.

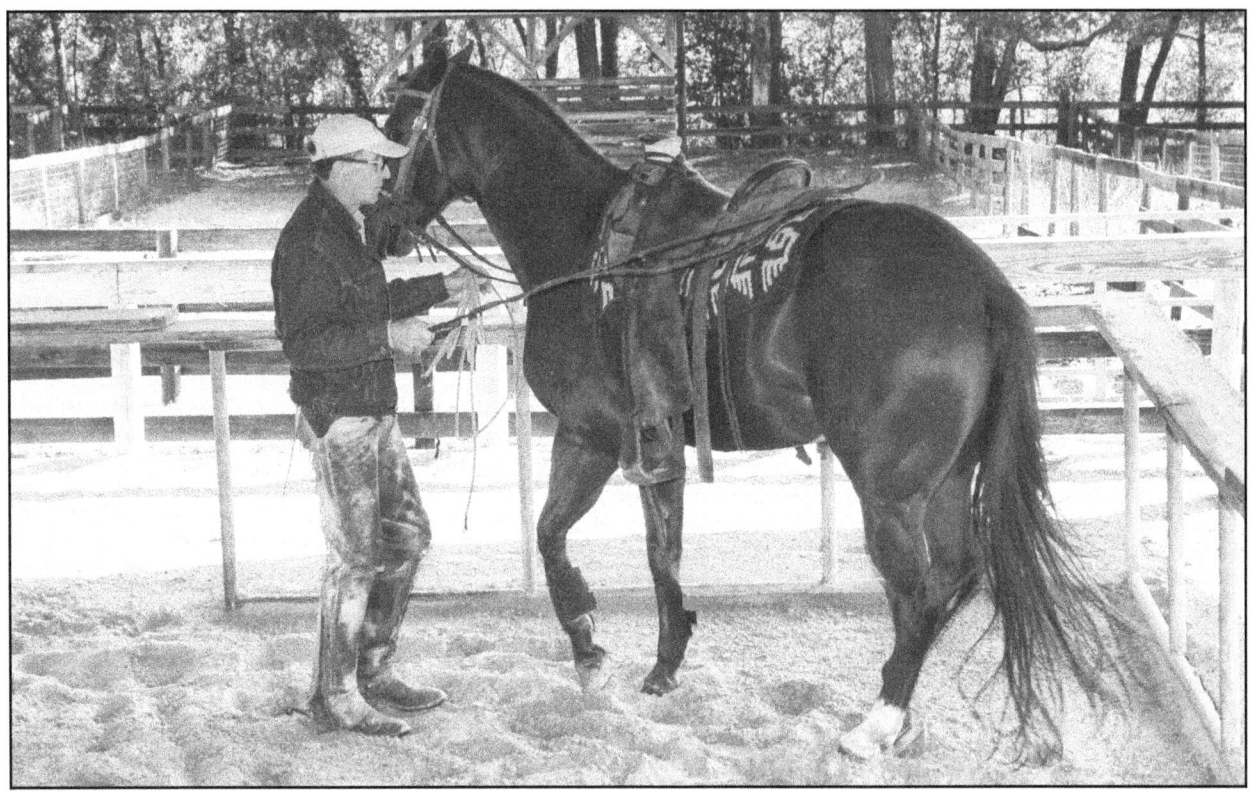

The Master Frank Barnett at work in the Post Pen (Square Pen).

MORE DEMANDING SUPPLING AND GYMNASTIC

In trot work, I ask the horse to move from one suppling or gymnastic exercise to another without loss of gait. An example of this is changing from shoulder-in to travers on a straight line of travel.

Let us say we are going to the left and I want to make that change. I bring my left leg forward to release the left hip back into alignment with the left front leg and I move my right lower leg back farther to ask the horse's hips to move into the arc in his body. As the hips move into the bend, I change my rein influence from holding the right shoulder to the left shoulder. That rein influence will be at the top of the horse's scapula and the horse makes the change in one stride. In time, it will be within the stride.

This is a pretty challenging transition for the horse because I am asking him to move from right diagonal balance left-hip-to-right-shoulder to left arc balance where the balance line moves down the center of his spine. I look for the horse to do it with fluidness and without hesitation in the gait. I also take this work out onto the circle.

Other combination work I use is right shoulder-in changing to a leg yield to the left. At some point on the diagonal line of travel in the leg yield, change back to a right shoulder-in on a straight line of travel. I also do this exercise from the left shoulder-in in the reverse.

An exercise I use a lot to help my turnaround work is a hip-in on a straight line, also known in French as travers. At first, I do it at the walk, but a walk with good energy. After 40 or 50 feet of travel, I pause the inside hind foot while still holding the hip-in *(see section on rein influences, chapter 8)*.

As the inside hind foot hesitates, the shoulders will move in the direction of the bend in the horse's body. This moves him off the straight line out onto the start of a circle. As soon as the shoulders start to move, I release the inside hind leg, and then, after a stride, pause it again. I repeat the pause to the inside hind leg while holding the hip-in until the horse has covered a 12-to-15 foot circle back to my original line of travel.

As we get back to the original line, I change the bend in his body toward the other way and do a hip-in, or travers, in the other direction again travelling for 40 or 50 feet. I again isolate the inside hind foot so that the shoulders move into the bend in his body.

If I do a hip-in to the left, I want to start to move the shoulders into the bend of his body. To do that, I put a slight backward motion on the right rein toward my belly button but not across the mane line of the horse. This will pause the left hind leg. At the same time, I hold my left rein at the top of the scapula to influence the shoulder to the left.

When the inside hind foot pauses, the right front leg of the horse will step in front of and across the left front leg. I don't want a big step to start with. I want it to take five-to seven pauses of the inside hind leg and that many movements of the shoulders to get back to my original line of travel. I usually do three sets on each end and then let the horse out of the movement.

When these 12-to-15 foot circles become good so that the horse can move with fluidness through the circle and re-bend for the other direction—always staying in the hip-in position without brace—I will start to trot the straight lines and break down to the walk just before influencing the inside hind leg. When this gets good, I start to put more hesitation on the hind leg so that the outside front leg moves farther across. This makes my circle smaller, and gets me back to my original line of travel with fewer steps. In time, the turn will be completely around the inside pivot foot and back onto the same line of travel in the other direction.

At some point, I will take this exercise into the round pen and do the hip-in right next to the rounded wall of the round-pen. When I bring the horse on the circle by pausing his inside hind leg to get back to my original line of travel, the horse will be looking into the wall, which increases the difficulty of the movement.

Taking hip-in, shoulder-in and shoulder-out into the round pen and doing them into the rounded wall of the pen where the horse is pushing into the solid curved barrier really raises the difficulty and gymnastic value of each exercise. It requires the horse to make a little extra move with his shoulder to re-balance as he is going forward looking into this barrier.

I won't go to the round pen with this work until it is very well established both on a straight line with good distance and on a circle. As this work proceeds in the round pen, my horse will reach a new level in his athletic abilities.

SIZE OF THE ROUND PEN

To do this work, the size of the round pen is important. I like 60 or 70 feet in diameter because it challenges the horse. At 80 feet or bigger, the arc of the wall is too shallow. Under 50 feet, the arc is too severe. Even a horse that is well-schooled will struggle going forward into these movements in a pen smaller than 50 feet.

A 50-to-60 foot round pen is great to use to work on the back-up. I can ask the horse to hold bend in his body to match the fence and make the slight adjustments with his hips as he backs around the pen. By now, I'm asking for a little speed in addition to fluidness in the steps. I don't want speed all the time but I want to bring the speed up, hold it for a number of strides, then let it slow down. Then speed it up again. I also do this on the straight back up.

Working the gate. This is to be done with speed and fluidness at its highest level. The horse should stay relaxed and controlled. It takes a number of years to develop a great gate horse. Mike Bridges riding Mud.

INTENSIFYING THE COW WORK

Now my horse has reached a level where he knows all aspects of his job to work cattle. He'll be better at some parts of the work than others. That is normal and I expect it. His ability to move his body and re-balance himself through those changes of positions has good speed and consistency.

He is now ready for me to ask him to step up to a higher level. I want to develop his full physical potential for quickness in answering my signals and changing from one position on the cow to the next.

One of the constants in working cattle is that you are not going to hold a position on the cow for long. You'll constantly change position relative to the different parts of the cow's body in order to hold mental domination over the cow so that it moves where you want it to go.

I like to start this work by separating cattle out of the rodear, or herd work. I'll ask my horse to stay in the herd for a long time, separating one cow right after the other. My body signals help; legs, pelvis and upper body signals are going to be smooth but very quick and with more energy. I'll bring the hackamore bars closer to the sides of the horse's face for faster hand signals.

Up to this point, I used the cow to help draw my horse from one position to the next. Now, I'm going to send my horse to the next position as soon as the cow's body indicates movement. By staying in the herd a long time and separating lots of cattle one after the other with a slightly higher signal intensity from me, my horse soon figures out that the quicker he dominates the cow, the quicker the cow leaves the herd, and the quicker he gets that little break. Then we go back into the herd to look for the next cow. In a short time, you will see the horses beating the cow to the next position.

Before, when it took three, four or five moves to dominate the cow mentally, my horse now gets it done in two or three moves. This does not happen all at once but builds over a period of repeated exercise with a higher level of intensity. It is very important that your horse has developed the ability to re-balance to a high degree. It's also important that he has the strength in his back to be able to work at this level of quickness. If you try to get there before the horse is physically and mentally ready, you may get more speed in the transitions from position to position on the cow, but you will also get bracing in the horse's body as he struggles to re-balance. This will come back to haunt you when your horse has to handle really tough cattle.

This horse has his head up with the cow, balancing a lot of weight over his hocks. The front end is light and ready to move. Ridden by Cheryl LeDoux at the Santucci Ranch, Prineville, OR

Remember, one of our primary goals in the development of this future bridle horse is to eliminate all braces in the body. This includes the natural bracing that comes about when the horse tests you and your program, and the bracing that comes about while schooling the horse in transitions up and down in gaits and changing from movement to movement as he learns how to re-balance through all these different transitions.

I'm writing this on a Sunday morning so I guess it is my day to preach. But I think this is a very important issue. I also use every opportunity when a cow is facing my horse to keep my horse square with the cow's eye. As the cow starts his move, I ask my horse to move his head in that same direction. If necessary, I'll have him move his body to shut that door on the cow. If the cow starts a move to her right, I want my horse to move his head and body enough to get his right eye past and beyond the cow's right eye. As the cow starts back to the left, I want my horse to instantly turn and move to the left and get his left eye past the cow's left eye. I ask my horse to hold that cow within a few feet of movement. I want him to keep shutting the door until the cow yields and moves directly away from my horse.

In time, and as the horse learns how to use this and as the opportunity presents itself, you will see your horse rock his head slightly from side-to-side while facing head-on to the cow, anticipating the cow's next move. He is also changing his eye from one side of the cow to the other to keep both doors closed until the cow yields away.

It's the nature of the horse to always hunt for the easiest way to do things. For the horse, the easy way is the one with the least expression of energy. Here we help him discover that he can trap a cow on the spot by using just the energy from one eye and very little movement from his body. This came about by making him be very quick to shut the door on the cow with a big move from his body that required a big burst of energy.

As this develops in a horse, it's a thrill to experience the feeling of your horse rock slightly from side to side with all that coiled-up power as he holds that cow in place with the energy from his eyes. When that happens, you know that your partner has reached another level and you helped him get there.

This horse has reached a high level where he can support a lot of weight over his hocks. His front end is light and the horse has good focus and intensity directed toward the heifer.

Rating the Cow's Speed

By now, we have headed some cattle at the run outside in the normal course of our work and we have probably practiced a little on the fence in the corral on slow cattle. It is the time to step it up.

Everything is in place for my horse mentally and physically. I like to have a pretty long fence because I want cattle with some speed.

I ask my horse to drive the cow down the fence, holding enough energy to the side of the cow to keep it on the fence. He must learn to rate the cow's speed and then answer the call to accelerate the front part of his body past the cow's eye to block the cow's forward travel. When the horse steps in to block the cow, he needs to make that block with bend, or arc, in his body and with his hip to the inside of the arc towards the cow. The step needs to be dramatic, with lots of openness in the horse's back. I want him to finish on his inside hind leg so he can roll back with the cow and send it up the same fence the other way.

If the block is made without bend in the horse's body and I go in straight, most of the time the cow will slip out behind my horse's hindquarters and will end up in the center of the pen. Then I'll have to bring her back to the fence to take her in the other direction.

When I make the block with arc in my horse's body, as the cow turns it sees and feels the energy from my horse's hip. I have the cow trapped in this cup of energy and that drives it back to the fence going the opposite direction.

All the groundwork and riding work I have done to develop my horse's ability to go forward, turnaround and stop with arc in his body is now going to pay off big time.

THE TEST OF SPEED

To test the quality of a training program, just add speed to the work. That will tell me how well my development work has been. If the horse can't do whatever I'm asking, without having to brace part or parts of his body, I'm not there yet and I'd better back up and do more development work.

Adding speed into all parts of my work at the right stage of development is important for my horse's confidence. I want him to know he can do it fast, and that at times he will be asked to do it fast. There will be times when we will need speed in order to get our jobs done.

Good blocking position by the horse in the stop. This leads to the horse being in position to make the next move. This shows great intensity.

The Cow's Pressure Zones

There are three pressure—or directional—zones on each side of the cow's body.

These are: 1) from the tailhead to the pin-bones to drive the cow forward, 2) from the pinbones to the shoulders for the cow to go forward but veer away from the source of pressure, and 3) from the middle of the shoulders to the eye of the cow for the stop and or turn.

Inside each of these directional zones is a whole series of little areas where the cow reacts to the energy delivered to that spot. What this amounts to is how a cow reads the horse's pressure, or energy, in that directional zone, and yields away. Of course, a lot of this depends on what the cow has learned from how it's been handled in the past and its personality. If I'm working a soft cow and want to drive it forward and yield slightly to the right, I position my horse's eye slightly ahead of the cow's flank on the left side. If it's a tough cow, the horse's eye position might be far forward on the ribcage but behind the cow's shoulder.

In heading a cow that I want to turn back into a fence or into the open, I drive my horse so his eye position is slightly ahead of the cow's eye, and set up the block. A lot of cattle will stop and turn when a horse's eye gets someplace past center of the cow's shoulders. The cow's point of reacting to the influencing pressure of the horse depends on how well the cow has been handled in the past and its personality. A horse and rider need to read this as it is happening and react to it.

(Note: The cow's balance point is the top center of its shoulders. The horse's balance point is the 14th thoracic vertebra. That is why a cow laying down will drop its hips to the ground first, and a horse will drop its shoulders first. This is the difference in the point of balance and re-balance.)

This horse is stopping with good hip engagement. The front end is light and the horse has good focus and intensity directed towards the heifer.

Up to this point in his development, I've been helping the horse to read and react to these differences in body position from cow to cow. Now it is time to start trusting him to read it and get there on his own. He is going to misread it at times and be late. I want to hang him out there and let him get himself into a little bit of trouble. At this stage, this horse knows how to dominate a cow. I want him to read more and more on his own with less help from me.

When he is late, I will help with my body signals, asking him to really hustle to make up for being late. Nature has given him the ability to read the cow much faster than I can. That is how he holds social position in his horse herd, by reading body language and reacting to it. I just need to open the door.

An extremely athletic move by the horse to get ahead of the heifer's eye. The horse's body is relaxed and the intensity is all on the cow. This horse has reached a high level of balance and the ability to rebalance. This is a reward for all the schooling work the two of you have done.

Chapter 8
FINISH WORK IN THE HACKAMORE

By now, my horse has completed his work in the 5/8-inch bosal, working through three changes of rope weight. With each change, he's becoming faster to the signals and lighter and quicker in his forequarters movements.

The last rope in the 5/8-inch bosal weighs one-and-one-eighth to $1^{1/4}$ pounds. I'm now ready for the 1/2-inch bosal. The finish work in the hackamore will involve only two ropes.

The first rope weighs one pound to $1^{1/8}$ pounds and the last rope will weigh about 3/4 to 7/8 of a pound. The bars of the bosal are snug to the horse's face. Consequently, even my slightest signals are very fast. These smaller size ropes don't have a lot of energy in them so everything needs to be understood by the horse. I am now relying more on my other body signals along with hand signals for this deeper understanding between us. Excellent balance and the ability to re-balance should be well-established. The physical braces in his body are gone. If one shows up, I address it and he releases it immediately.

Everything is right in this picture.
Dusty is ready to move up to the 1/2 inch bosal.

The horse's mental focus is with me more than not. He is relaxed emotionally, comfortable with the work, understands faster signals because of the work I've done as we progressed through the change of rope weights and bosal sizes.

SPEED OF THE SIGNALS

I started with the bars of the bigger bosal away from his face. This results in a slower signal with some lag time for the horse to get mentally prepared. Being patient and building toward faster bar signals as I reduce rope weight and bosal size will now pay off big time because my horse will understand and be able to handle the very fast signal. The faster he can understand the signal and remain balanced, the shorter the distance my hands have to move. I'm really going to need that later in the two-rein work when I put the horse into the bridle, and farther down the road when I ride him straight in the bridle.

For the finish work in the hackamore, I don't use a bosal smaller than 1/2-inch. The 3/8-inch and 5/16-inch bosals used for the two-rein work are too small. This is because their cores don't have enough resiliency if you use it like a regular hackamore. In a short time, they will get too soft and raggy.

In the two-rein work, the bars of these smaller bosals are under the bridle hanger or headstall and, consequently, their movement is limited. So we ask the horse to read the bar signals a little differently. I'll discuss this more in the next chapter.

The 1/2-inch bosal I use for this work will be 10-to-11$^{1/2}$ inches long and have very little heel weight. Some horses with large muzzles need a 12-inch bosal.

I personally prefer a bosal with 16-plait or more on the bars. In this discipline, I use the finer braided bar with the change to the 5/8-inch bosal and continue with this finer braid with the 1/2-inch bosal. This finer braided bar is part of the process for my horse to understand and answer a signal with less energy. A 16-plait bar has less bite to it than a 12-plait bar.

I'll continue with all the work I've done up to this point. I'll ask my horse to continue becoming faster with this smaller bar size and less weight. In addition, I'll start to ride the schooling work and the cow work in one hand as preparation for my two-rein work. I'm not going to ride with one hand all the time but will add it in as we do our work. First, we'll ride the simpler exercises with one hand and, as time goes by, do more and more.

Left shoulder-out. This shows nice frame and movement.

Left travers or hip-in. This shows nice frame and movement by the horse. Mud is being ridden in a 1/2 inch bosal and a 3/4 pound rope. The reins show good contact along with lightness. Notice the slight drop on the inside rein.

Right shoulder-in. The horse shows good frame and good movement.

Rein Influences

Riding in the two-rein is a big mental transition for the horse. He has to start reading more of the rein signal from the indirect rein when both reins are in one hand.

It is easy to teach the horse to understand rein signals when we ride them in two hands, with one hand moving the direct rein. The direct rein is the one on the same side of the horse as the direction of movement. The other hand moves the indirect—or supporting—rein. That's the rein on the side of the horse away from the direction of movement. On a horse moving to the left, it would be the right rein.

Each rein influences the opposite hind foot because a horse's primary balance is on the diagonal. The left rein influences the left front leg and the right hind leg. Correspondingly, the right rein influences the right front leg and left hind leg.

When we start to ride in one hand and ask the horse for work that requires some frame, or openness in the back, it's quite a mental transition for the horse to read most of the hand signal off of one rein. This is the start of that process.

I begin this introduction to one-hand reining with a loop in my reins. I'll hold the reins in my left hand with my knuckles up toward the sky. This gives me quite a bit of spread between the reins. When I move my hands left or right, I will still give the horse some direct rein influence along with indirect rein influence. As we progress in the work, I can introduce more indirect rein by how much I cant, or tip, my hand off of level.

If I ask my horse to go left, I move my left hand to the left from home base with my knuckles flat, or level, across the top. That still leaves quite a bit of direct rein influence along with indirect rein. In that same move, if I cant my left hand so that the knuckle on my little finger is pointing down toward the horse's mane or shoulder before I move it from home base, I will have a lot of indirect influence and very little direct rein influence.

Every degree of cant in the rein hand, from flat across the top to the little finger knuckle pointing straight down, will affect how much indirect rein you ask the horse to understand and respond to.

The horse can sort out these signal changes if they are done correctly and with patience on the rider's part. All too often we see horses being reined in one hand and being asked to go left or right with the horse bracing his jaw in the opposite direction. That immediately leads to bracing in the horse's back and the quality of the movement falls apart.

In asking the horse to go right from this same hand position, the effect of the hand is the same. If I move my left rein hand to the right from home base, there is more influence on the left rein against the horse's neck and less influence to the right rein, which stays a little passive.

I keep building this into my work, with both real work time and schooling time. I begin with the slower, easier movements and, gradually, move into the speed work. I always keep track of where my horse is mentally and physically. It is very important that I take the time to get this part understood by the horse before moving on. If I don't, it will come back to haunt me when I ride him in the two-rein or straight up in the bridle.

The next step for me in this one-hand reining with the 1/2-inch bosal is to hold the reins together in a closed hand with my knuckles toward the ears of the horse. This is the same position I ride the horse in the bridle bit. In order to influence the indirect rein, the effect of the hand is all in the cant on the bottom part of the hand for either left or right.

There is very little direct rein influence in this hand position. At times, if my horse needs some direct rein help, I'll reach above my closed rein hand with my right hand to shorten the inside rein at the top of the loop.

I ride with my left hand in these one-hand positions because I rope with my right hand and arm. If I was a left-handed roper, it would be reversed. I think it's good to practice riding using your non-dominant bridle hand so that you build muscle memory for both sides of your body.

The time it takes to get through this finish work in the hackamore varies greatly from horse to horse. It could take one-to-two years before I feel he's ready for the two-rein work. My total time to develop him to this point could be four-to-six years. Once at this point, he is a pretty fancy horse in his work, one I would be proud to ride into somebody else's cow camp.

THE FINISHED PRODUCT

By the end of the 1/2-inch hackamore finish work, I have everything on my horse that he needs to do his job with a high level of balance and speed of movement. The only reason to go further into the two-rein work, and then straight up in the bridle, is to get all of this great movement into one hand with more speed in the horse and with less movement of the rider's hand. The communication between the horse and rider's body becomes subtle nuances, even with speed and quickness in the work.

There will be times when I will come back to the 1/2-inch hackamore in the horse's working life once we are in the bridling process. For instance, if it is a day I'm going to work in heavy brush, I will ride him in the 1/2-inch so I don't take a chance of the brush hanging up in the bridle reins and jerking his mouth. Or, on extremely cold days, I will keep the iron out of his mouth.

By this point, he is finished in the hackamore. He and I have both done our work and have taken the time to make it right. It is all there. I can always come back to the 1/2-inch hackamore during the two-rein work or after he's straight up in the bridle. From now until the day one of us dies, he has reached a new plateau.

Chapter 9
The Two-Rein Bosal ~ How it Works

The two-rein bosal I use to help the horse through the bridling process is a hackamore set-up consisting of a bosal (3/8-inch or 5/16-inch bar size) with a lightweight hanger and a horsehair rope rein of the same diameter size. The rein is usually four or six strands.

This can be referred to either as a "two-rein bosal" or a "two-rein hackamore." I refer to it as a two-rein bosal to give it a distinct name separate from our bigger hackamores.

The larger bosals used in the hackamore process to get the horse to this point in his education operate principally in two ways: by rotation of the nose button, and through the bar signals that move into the side of the horse's face. Even as we tighten the bars closer to the face, the bar signal is still a sideways movement against the horse's face.

In using the two-rein bosal under the bridle headstall, there is very restricted movement of the bars of the bosal. The nose rotation is the same, however, and radiates energy over a wide area because the two-rein bosal fits snug to the face of the horse. The bars of the bosal are also snug to the sides of the face.

Tightening what's called the "whooie" knot (a half-hitch) on my rein rope, I bring the bars in more toward the jawbone of the horse to a point where they have influence on the lower lip muscles of the horse. This creates a very fast bar signal. I set the bars of the two-rein bosal so that they touch these two lip muscles but don't pinch them.

The lower lip muscles are located on the sides of the horse's face between the curve groove of the lip and the bone of the jaw that you can feel under the skin. They will feel like a cord, the size of a wood pencil or an ink pen.

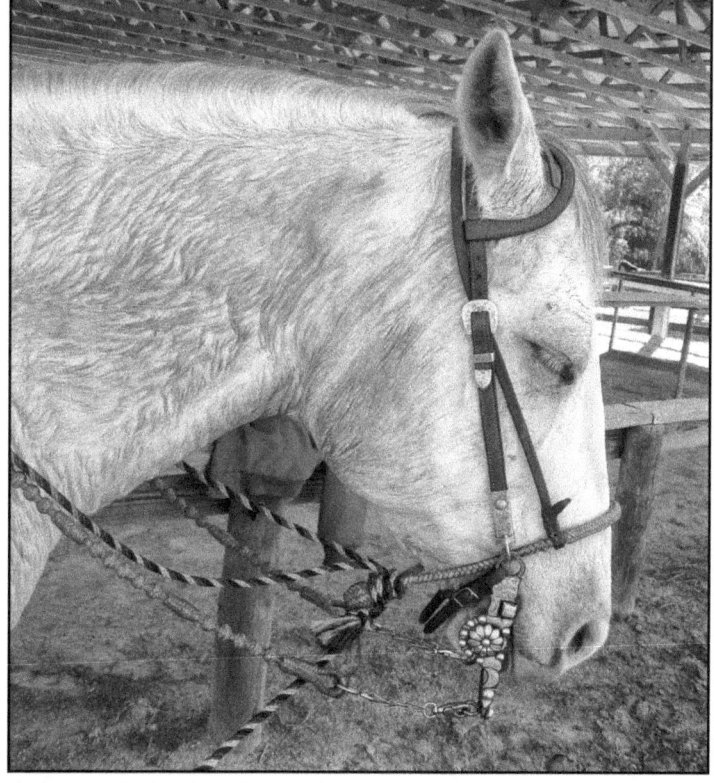

A close-up look at how the small bosal fits under the bridle headstall. When you are talking about riding a horse in the two-rein, you are referring to all the equipment you see here. The small bosal is usually 3/8 or 5/16 inch in size with a light-weight head hanger. The reins attached to the bosal are around 1/4 to 1/2 pound in weight. Next is the bridle bit that has a one piece cannon, along with a headstall, chin strap and a set of reins. The reins are traditionally made as one continuous piece of rawhide with a romal attached as a counter-weight.

Adding Hand Signals

By now, my horse is ready for this speed of signal because I have developed it through the training. He can now balance and re-balance within the stride, whatever work we are doing.

I need these fast positive hand signals at this stage of starting the horse into the bridle. That's because I am now limited to how far my hands can move laterally left and right from the center of the neck of the horse before I have an adverse effect on the bridle bit in his mouth.

I refer to this area for good hand movement as the "bridle box." It starts above the fork of the saddle and is about 11 inches long from the fork toward the horse's ears and is about seven inches wide, that is, about $3^{1/2}$ inches on either side of the horse's mane. If the bridle reins move outside this "bridle box," it will start to tilt the bridle bit in the horse's mouth. This compresses his tongue toward the bars of his mouth which causes him to brace his jaw in the opposite direction from the side you are asking him to bend or move.

There are advantages to using the two-rein bosal to help the horse learn to read almost all signals of the indirect rein to achieve the various movements I'll ask of him. I don't have to disturb the horse's mouth as he learns to support the bridle bit with his tongue and hard palate. I can spread the bosal reins for more direct or indirect influence without tilting the bridle bit in the horse's mouth.

When a horse is "straight-bridled," all signals or corrections involve the mouth. "Straight-bridled" refers to a horse that has been transitioned from the hackamore or snaffle bit into a bridle bit without using the two-rein bosal. The lack of good physical and mental confidence by the horse can lead to bracing in the jaw, poll and, subsequently, in the horse's back. I have straight-bridled a few horses and they turned out all right. However, all of them had some little braces at the end of the process that I put in there by being in his mouth before there was good mental confidence.

If you put your fingers between the bridle reins, you will tilt the bit in the horse's mouth. In this discipline, I ride with my hand closed around the bridle reins. I never put a finger between them. With the two-rein bosal, I can develop the horse's understanding of indirect rein signals or do rein corrections without being in his mouth. I tie the hair rope reins of the two-rein bosal the same as the reins of the bigger hackamores. Like those, I don't want more than four wraps behind

The horse is being ridden in the two-rein set-up. The hackamore rein is ahead of the bridle rein. This puts it first as the primary signaling rein. The hand position on the hackamore rein would be referred to as a two-finger spread.

the reins and the "whooie" knot. I would really like to have a two-rein bosal that required just one-to-three wraps for less heel weight.

The less heel weight the better for these super fast signals. I don't need a lot of weight for a signal release. The bosal is snug to the face. The activating signals are slight movements, and the release of that signal is very subtle.

With the two-rein bosal tied, I fit it to the horse's face. I want the bars of the bosal to be above the curve groove of the lip where there is a slight hollow area on most horses. This gives it room under the headstall. On some bridle bits, I flair the hanger holes slightly to the outside. This is to increase the freedom of movement for the bridle bit so that it doesn't drag along the bars of the bosal.

Positioning the bars of the bosal in this hollow area may put your nose button down lower on the face than where your sweet spot is for the bigger hackamore. For most horses, this is not a problem. They understand the rotation of the nose button and will respond with speed. If my horse doesn't respond to the nose button with the speed I think he should, I will have to move back up to his sweet spot. That will require a longer bosal. But that may make it more difficult to influence the lower lip muscles with the bars of the bosal.

When I hang the two-rein bosal so that there's a lot of angle to it from the nose button to the heel knot, the other muscles on the sides of the horse's face can bulge out enough that it can make it difficult to bring the bars back in to influence those two cord like muscles. I will have some understanding and response to the bar signals, but the fastest bar signals come from those lower lip muscles, and that is what I am after; speed with understanding.

How I use my hand or hands to operate this two-rein bosal, I will save for a later chapter. There are some other things we should consider and understand before starting to ride with the two-rein bosal and the bridle bit.

Chapter 10
THE HORSE'S MOUTH

Horses' mouths can vary greatly from one horse to the next. They all have the same parts: teeth, tongue, hard and soft palate and the diastema or, as it is commonly referred to, the bar of the mouth.

From horse to horse, these parts can be longer, shorter, thicker, thinner, different shape in configuration, and there can be more or less teeth. As a bridle horseman, these are things I need to understand.

TEETH AND DENTAL CARE

Before discussing the different parts of the mouth and how they relate to the bridling process, let me talk about dental care for the horse's mouth. Continuous good dental care is extremely important if high performance is wanted from our horses. If I bend my horse to the right, or ask him to move right, his lower jaw needs to articulate to the left. If I ask him to bend or go left, this is reversed and his jaw needs to articulate to the right. When his face comes toward the vertical, the lower jaw needs to move down slightly.

If there is ridging on the table top of the teeth, hooks or misalignment of the table for the molars and incisor teeth, the horse will have to open his mouth to articulate his jaw.

Most of the mouthing problems I see are teeth-related. They immediately cause bracing in the jaw, poll and then to the back of the horse.

Teeth problems in horses are more prevalent today than they were 2,000 years ago, or even 200 years ago. Horse teeth are designed to grow continuously. The action of biting grass or other plant material and then grinding it is what is supposed to keep the tables of the teeth worn down and at the proper angle.

The way we feed horses, and the grasses we have today, does not promote that. For that to happen, the horse, in his natural environment, would have to eat about 17 hours a day. That grazing may not be continuous but more time is spent eating than doing anything else.

Today, if we keep horses confined, we feed them two or three times a day. For the horse, that amounts to fewer hours of grinding feed. Even if your horse is turned out to pasture, the grasses we have today have less silica in them than most of the older grass varieties. Consequently, today we feed horses softer and less abrasive types of feed that allows them to make a shorter stroke with the molars in grinding their food.

This shorter stroke of the molars across each other promotes ridging on the outside edge of the teeth which leads to an incorrect angle of the molar tables. It can—and will—get to a point where the jaw cannot articulate without the horse opening his mouth. This leads to mental stress and the braces we talked about earlier.

The vaquero-style bridle horse is supposed to have a very quiet and soft mouth while he is doing his work, regardless of the speed of the work. Consequently, I have my horses' teeth checked twice a year. I think every horse needs to be checked at least once a year.

As a bridle horseman, I want to know what each individual horse's mouth looks like on the inside. This gives me a much better idea of what bits have a better chance of fitting into the mouth with comfort and those that probably won't. Configuration of the mouth and the personality of the horse play a big part in this.

Examining the Parts

When we first look at the horse's mouth from the outside, we see the lips. On 99 out of 100 horses, the space from the curve groove to the end of the lips gives you an indication of the length of the mouth from the incisors to the molars. What you see on the outside will represent the length of the mouth where the horse will hold the bridle bit.

I prefer a short mouth over a long mouth for the use of a leverage bit. With the short mouth, the point of "transitioning rotation" is closer to the end of the nose than it is in a long mouth. With a signal bit, it doesn't make any difference because you are up high enough in the mouth where the hard palate is raising away from the tongue. The port of the bit is operating between two different surfaces; the tongue and the hard palate.

When I open up the horse's mouth, I look at the thickness of the tongue. A thick tongue has more mass to support the cannon of the bit. With that support, there will be more distance from the cannon of the bit to the bar of the mouth.

I don't want my bit to be on the bars of the horse's mouth. With a thinner tongue, I will try a bit with a mouthpiece that has a little tongue relief in the cannon. This can help him get more configuration in his tongue to help support the bit against the hard palate. The tongue is a very strong muscle that naturally rests in the horse's mouth except when he extends it or pulls it back up to shut the air flap so he can swallow. Just like the human, the horse doesn't move around with his tongue hanging out of his mouth. He keeps it pulled back into his mouth behind his incisor teeth with some tension in it.

This natural ability to hold tension in his tongue makes it easy for the horse to support a bridle bit using his tongue and the surface of his hard palate for long periods of time. This is possible as soon as he learns to configure his tongue to the cannon and port of the particular bit.

Mentally and physically, it takes some time for the horse to reach a point when he can support the bridle bit with complete confidence through transitions and movements. I believe it takes more mental confidence for the horse than physical strength of the tongue.

The hard palate in the roof of the mouth plays a role in the horse's ability to support the bridle bit, especially in the lower port leverage bits. As the horse picks up the bit with its tongue, he configures his tongue for the cannon and the back of the port and pushes the port of the bit to his hard palate to help support it.

When you look at the hard palate in a horse's mouth, the soft tissue comes in three general shapes: flat with ridges, shaped like the top of a pipe with ridges, or shaped like a teepee tent with ridges and narrow at the top. Within each of these general shapes, there are hundreds of variations.

If I had a horse with a hard palate shaped like a teepee tent and I chose a bridle bit with a wide flat port, it wouldn't fit well to the hard palate and could cause undue pressure. That could lead to mental stress. That's why there are so many different styles of ports in the vaquero bridle bits.

The male horse generally has 40 teeth in his mouth. The female horse has 36 teeth. The four teeth that are different are the canine teeth, which are also referred to as the bridle teeth. There are usually two in the upper jaw and two in the lower jaw. Bridle teeth can be in different parts of the gum line from horse to horse and interfere with the bridling process if they are too high up toward the molars in the upper jaw.

Even if they don't physically interfere with the bridle bit, canine teeth can get very sharp and have a tendency to stick into the tongue as the horse is picking up the bit to support it. They need to be cut off and polished like a pearl. This should also be done with the bottom ones as well so they don't interfere with the unbridling process.

About 40-to-60 percent of horses will also have what are referred to as "wolf teeth" in the upper and/or lower gum line, just ahead of the first molars. These teeth are quite brittle and can break above the gum line with the use of a snaffle bit or a bridle bit and, so, should be removed. If they fracture above the gum line and are still protruding into the mouth, the bit getting up against them and moving them around will inflame the soft tissue and cause the horse to get a very sore mouth.

The mouth of the horse is one of its parts we use for communication. I influence the mouth to indicate direction of movement and to bring the horse from a passive rein back into my hands as I engage his hips to open his back. Paying attention to all parts of the mouth gives me a better chance to pick a bridle bit that will fit that mouth and start to build understanding and confidence in the horse right from the start of the bridling process.

Chapter 11
VAQUERO-STYLE BRIDLE BITS

Bridle bits have been around for a long time, at least 6,000 years in one form or another. The first ones were made from bone, then iron and probably other materials that did not pass the test of time. All of them were originally designed as instruments of leverage to control forward motion in the horse.

When I refer to a bridle bit, I'm talking about a bit that has a solid mouthpiece as opposed to a bit that is hinged in the middle or hinged in two or more places. Those would be the snaffle bit, or a form thereof called correction bits or training bits.

The type of bridle bits that we are concerned with are the ones used by the vaqueros and buckaroos in the western United States. These have evolved over the last 480 years to what they are today.

LASTING HISTORY

Some of the cheek piece and mouthpiece designs we use in this discipline today came from the Iberian Peninsula in Spain with the conquistadors and, later, with Spanish immigrants to Mexico and what was referred to as Alta California. They reflect a strong Moorish influence because of the domination of most of Spain for 800 years by the Moors.

We also have newer-designed cheek pieces and mouthpieces that were developed here by horsemen seeking the best bit for a particular horse. Some of these bridle bits have endured because it was found the newer mouthpieces fit well into a particular configuration of a horse's mouth, whether flat palate, rounded or teepee-shaped, as well as having either thin or thick tongues.

Cheek pieces were modified to enhance the action of the mouthpieces, either by speeding up their movement or slowing them down.

HOW THE BIT WORKS

No bit is severe; only humans are severe. Bridle bits are either fast or slow, meaning one bit will come to leverage faster or more slowly than another. That depends on how the bit is engineered. Most cheek pieces on the bits in this discipline are built at a two-to-one or a two-and-a-half-to-one ratio, or a combination between these measurements.

If the cheek is constructed at a two-to-one ratio, it means it will be measured by taking one measurement from the center of the cannon to the top of the hanger hole. Then a second measurement is taken from the center of the cannon to the point of pull at the bottom of the cheek piece. The second measurement would be twice that of the top measurement.

If two bridle bits have the same cheek piece design and one is built at a ratio of two-to-one and the other is at a ratio of two-and-a-half-to-one, the second will come to leverage faster. Leverage is applied through the chin strap at the jawbone of the horse.

What this means for the rider is that the shorter the distance your rein hand must move for the signal to get to your horse, the faster the bit. In other words, for leverage to take place, the less your hand has to move.

People have discussed and written about leverage bridle bits for a long time and referred to their action as "fulcrum leverage." In the past, I have referred to how they work the same way.

When I spoke about leverage bits, I referred to the ones built at a higher ratio, like two-and-a-half-to-one, as being faster for the horse to respond to the movement of the rider's hand, and that the rider's hand would have less distance to travel. It also takes less pressure on the reins to get that response. This is what I felt in my hand with the horses I've put into the bridle.

The True Mechanics of the Bridle Bit

About 17 years ago, I met a writer who was interested in writing an article about me and the California-style bridle horse. At one point in our discussion, she told me that my statement that my hand would move less with less pressure for a higher ratio bit in order to get the horse to respond was incorrect as it related to fulcrum leverage.

She said the mechanical laws of fulcrum leverage dictate that a higher ratio would move faster but would require more pressure to move it. I told her that was not what I was feeling in my hand and that it did move less and took less pressure. She said that was not a good enough explanation and she was uncomfortable with it. If I could not prove it, she said, she was not going to write the article.

Feel is a very elusive thing to explain and, at the time, that was all I had. So we agreed to disagree. Yet her questions kept haunting me. So I decided to try to find some help to determine whether I was right or wrong in my explanation.

Over the next two years, I took my question to five engineers and a master toolmaker. Three of the engineers said what was going on was fulcrum leverage. One engineer said there was more going on than just fulcrum leverage but he couldn't explain it. The master toolmaker thought more was happening than fulcrum leverage but he couldn't explain it, either. At this point, I was getting pretty frustrated.

Then, through a friend, I met a man who was willing to spend some time with me. He is a mechanical design engineer for the two biggest engineering research labs in the United States. After going through the processes with him, he said that these bridle bits we were looking at were not creating pure fulcrum leverage in the horse's mouth. Instead, he said, the leverage taking place should be referred to as "transitioning-rotation."

He explained that the part of the bit in the horse's mouth—the port and the cannon—raises slightly as the bit is moved from the pressure applied through the reins. This creates energy that is transmitted from the cannon in the horse's mouth up and forward in an arc, and then back toward the chin strap. He also said that everything associated with the bit would have an effect on the shape of that arc; the density of the tongue, the shape of the cheek piece and the ratio it was built to, the weight of the reins between the hand and the bit, the thickness and width of the headstall, and where it is attached to the bit.

A nice example of California Hangers

When he made the statement about the headstall attachment, a light switched on in my head. I asked him if he thought that a very narrow attachment to the bridle hanger would be better. He said that would have the least amount of disruptive influence during this transitioning-rotation. I told him about the California Hanger which is a metal end put on the end of the headstall with a very thin metal strap that goes through the hanger holes of the bridle bit. I have seen California Hangers for as long as I can remember. I always thought they were more of a fiesta thing to create a look. I knew I should have asked! Those old-timers had it figured out a long time ago, and I'm sure they did not have a lot of mathematical or engineering skills. They did it through feel.

The more mass you move, the more energy it creates in this transitioning-rotation.

I believe this is a contributing factor in the higher port bits for the amount of feel you get back into your hand, along with the port of the bit touching more area of the sensitive tissues in the mouth of the horse.

Cheek pieces that are swept back at the end of the shank where the reins attach will be slower than a straight cheek piece if everything else is equal and both are built at the same ratio. Some horses need this slower movement, depending on their mental make-up, especially at the first part of the bridling process. Later, as their confidence builds, they can handle a faster bit.

We see many different types of mouthpieces or ports in these vaquero-type bridle bits, from low ports, through medium range, to very high ports, and for good reason. Every horse's mouth is different in physical configuration; long mouth, short mouth, thick tongue, thin tongue, bridle teeth spacing in the male horse, and shape of the palate. Along with these physical differences is the mental make-up of the individual horse.

The horse must support the mouthpiece with his tongue and, for the process to be successful, the horse must gain complete confidence. The mouthpiece or port moves in the horse's mouth as the bit moves toward leverage, creating feel in the horse's mouth. As it comes to leverage, it adds compression to the tongue. These two things send feel back to your rein hand when a bridle bit is used as a leverage instrument.

The mouthpieces or ports in these bridle bits are either forward-hung in the cheek or center-hung. The forward-hung mouthpiece will compress the tongue more slowly at leverage than the center-hung. Straight bar mouthpieces will put the pressure evenly across the face of the tongue. A mouthpiece with tongue relief (indented space in the center of the bridle bar) will apply more pressure on each side of the tongue and less in the center.

The balance of the bridle bit is determined by a combination of the cheek piece and the mouthpiece used, and at what angle the mouthpiece is set into the cheek. It will be balanced either forward of or behind center.

Development of the Signal Bit

At some point in the evolution of the vaquero discipline or even before, some horsemen who felt the schooling of a horse to be an art form found that with a high enough port that would sit far up in the horse's mouth, where there is space between the tongue and the palate, the horse had a chance to respond to the lifting of the port from the tongue *before* leverage takes place.

When a horse is given the chance to respond to this signal and finds it, he can be operated with mere ounces of pressure and the slightest of hand movement, hence the term "signal bit bridle horse."

There are very few mouthpieces with which this can be accomplished. The spade bit is the one most used and also the most misunderstood bit in the world. Most people think the spade bit to be very cruel or severe when, in fact, it is designed to operate with the least amount of movement and pressure.

The discipline that evolved using these styles of bits requires only intermittent contact with the bridle bit and mouth of the horse. It probably came about as the horse was transformed from war horse to cow horse. The long hours of moving cattle or holding cattle to be worked didn't require the vaquero to move his horse on the collected rein. However, when he needed to perform with some degree of collection, like separating cattle from the herd or roping, the bridle reins were shortened, thus sending a signal to the horse's mouth to create feel. The horse responded to the rider's hand, staying there until released.

It must be remembered that the bridle bit in and of itself does not make a great horse. It is a signaling device to enhance our hand movements. We must ride our horses with all of our body.

Here are some of the bridle bits used in this discipline. My opinion about them is based on my experience using them on different horses.

Bridle Bits

1. Salinas mouthpiece without a hood over the port with a modified Santa Paula cheek – This is a leverage bit. It's very easy for most horses to pick up with their tongues because it has a slight amount of tongue relief.

2. Fat Frog mouthpiece that is forward-hung, with a modified U.S. shank – This is one of at least eight different Frog mouthpieces that range in port height from low like this one up to one that can signal.

3. MAC mouthpiece with Hash Knife cheek – This is a leverage bit that does not give me much feel back into my hand but has become my favorite two-rein bit at the start of the process. Low port bridle bits don't create very much feel in the horse's mouth or back to the rider's hands because they are encased in soft tissue, the tongue and the palate. As you move up in the horse's mouth toward the back of the jaw, there is more room between these two areas, giving the higher ports a chance for more movement, which creates more feel. I have yet to find a horse with a clean mouth in the United States or Europe that will not pick up this bit. If I have a horse in the Bridle Clinic that has had bitting problems, he or she is going to get this bit at the start. A horse must hold a bit with some confidence before you can start to repair the mind.

Bridle Bits, cont.

4. Salinas mouthpiece with a standard Santa Barbara cheek – This is a leverage bit, easy for most horses to pick up. It has a small amount of tongue relief. This mouthpiece sits at an angle in the cheek pieces so the horse's tongue can support the whole backside of the port as he picks it up and pushes it to the palate.

5. Polo mouthpiece with a modified Santa Paula cheek – (This is modified from the original check design). This leverage bit gives almost no feel back to your hands and has no tongue relief (very little mass for movement to create feel between the tongue and the palate).

6. Standard Santa Barbara cheek with a Spanish Spade mouthpiece – This bit can be used as a signal bit or a leverage bit. I've used the bit for more than 30 years.

7. Standard Santa Barbara cheek with a San Joaquin mouthpiece – This is a leverage bit. It can be made high enough to be operated as a signal bit if the port is as high as the top of the hanger holes on the cheek pieces. Even as a leverage bit, a horse can give a lot of feel back to your hand.

8. Short Santa Barbara cheek with a Spoon Spade – This bit can operate as a signal bit or a leverage bit, creating lots of feel in your hand. The configuration of the horse's mouth and tongue will determine whether a Spanish Spade or a Spoon Spade will give the best results. The Spoon Spade is generally made shorter than the Spanish Spade. You want the upper part of the port to sit where the most room is between the tongue and palate. The long mouthed horse might need the Spanish Spade; the short-mouthed horse will need the Spoon Spade. However, this is not cast in stone.

9. Hill Frog mouthpiece with a standard Santa Barbara cheek – This is a leverage bit that gives a lot of feel back into your hand. The port is high enough to reach the area of the mouth where you start to get more space between the tongue and palate.

Bridle Bits, cont.

10. A Fat Frog mouthpiece with a modified Santa Paula cheek – This leverage bit can be useful on older horses that have been pulled on, if you are trying to re-bridle them and repair the mental and physical damage. This mouthpiece gives more bearing surface for the tongue to support. It spreads the compression of the tongue over a wider area, which gives a softer feel. As the bit comes to leverage this can be helpful.

11. Standard Santa Barbara cheek with a Spanish Spade mouthpiece – This bit can operate as a signal bit or a leverage bit with a lot of feel back to your hand. I've used this bit for more than 35 years. It has been rebuilt and needs it again. It is getting so loose that the speed of the bit is slow and my hand signal has to move more than it should.

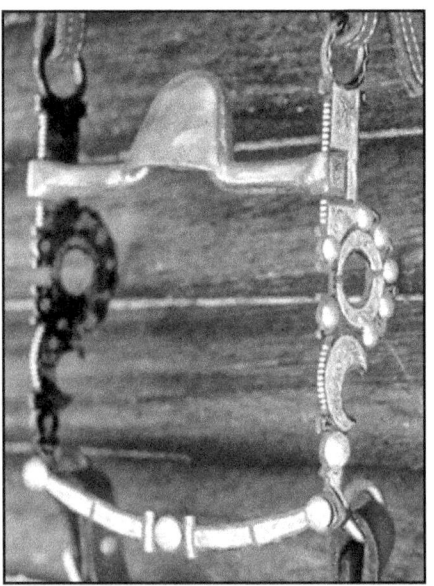

12. Santa Barbara cheek with a Salinas mouthpiece – This is a fast leverage bit. Most horses can easily pick up this mouthpiece. It sits in the lower part of the mouth where the tongue and palate are close together.

13. A Mullen Polo mouthpiece with a Visalia cheek – Mullen means the bar of the mouthpiece is concave. This is a leverage bit. The mouthpiece being mullened causes it to sit more on the outside edge of the tongue. This will compress the tongue faster as the bit comes to leverage. It is designed to get to the bars of the horse's mouth faster than a straight mouthpiece. The bars in the mouth are not where I want to operate. I want the horse to respond before the tongue is compressed that far.

14. Salinas mouthpiece with a Santa Paula cheek – This is a nice leverage bit that is easy for most horses to pick up at the start of the bridling process. This mouthpiece sits at an angle in the cheek pieces so the horse's tongue can support the whole backside of the port, as he picks it up and pushes it to the palate.

15. A 25 or 27 mouth very similar to a Salinas with a standard Santa Barbara cheek – These are catalog numbers. The proper name for this is unknown. The sides of the port are straighter than the Salinas and give me more feel back into my hand. The cheeks are Santa Barbara and this bit is a leverage bit.

Bridle Bits, cont.

16. San Joaquin mouthpiece with a Big Santa Barbara cheek – This is a signal bit. I use the big Santa Barbara cheeks (more mass and weight) after the horse has attained a high degree of confidence in supporting a bridle bit if I want to help him find some self-carriage. There is a point when a horse breaks at the poll and is supports a bridle bit with his tongue. The weight of the bit is hanging from his poll and there is no weight in his mouth. Once the horse finds self-carriage, he will keep hunting for it. Over time, he will develop that classic bridle horse look with no pressure on the reins. This image of the horse with his poll flexed and face on the vertical is very pleasing to the bridle horseman. Especially, if the horse has achieved self-carriage with no pressure on the reins. Self-carriage can also be achieved with a hackamore. If it is done at that stage of schooling, the horse will find it faster during the bridling process.

17. Modified Half-Breed with a big Santa Barbara cheek – This is a leverage bit with a lot of feel. A modified Half-Breed is a reduced variation of the true Half-Breed, which is the base that the spade is built on. Usually having a lower and wider port than the true Half-Breed.

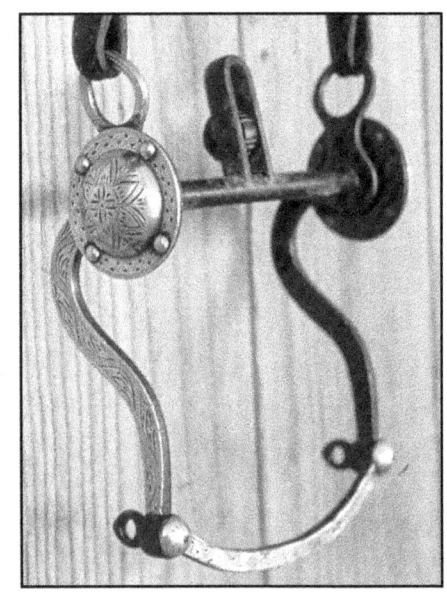

18. Traditional Half-Breed mouthpiece with U.S. cheek –This bit can be a signal bit or a leverage bit. The traditional Half-Breed is the base that the spade is set on when it is built. When the spade is left off, it can work as a signal bit if it is at least as high as the top of the hanger holes.

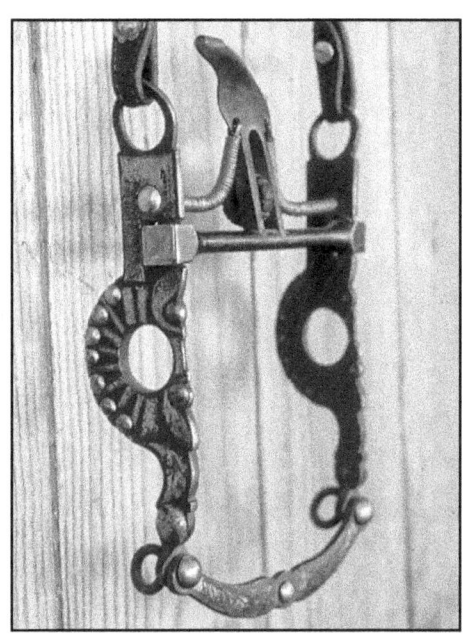

19. Spanish Spade mouthpiece with Big Santa Barbara cheeks – This bit will operate as a signal bit or a leverage bit. Either way, you are going to get a lot of feel back into your hands. The mass of the mouthpiece creates a lot of feel between the soft tissues of the tongue and palate.

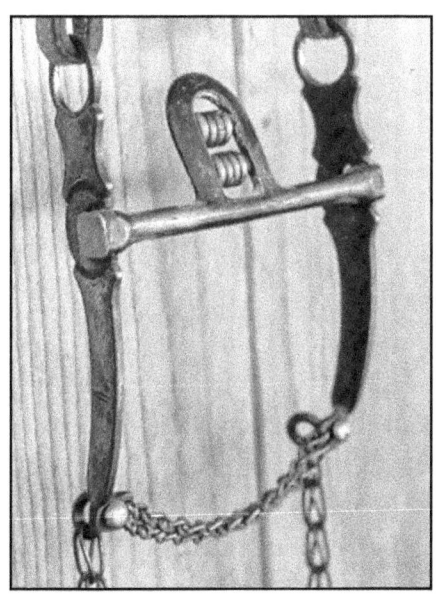

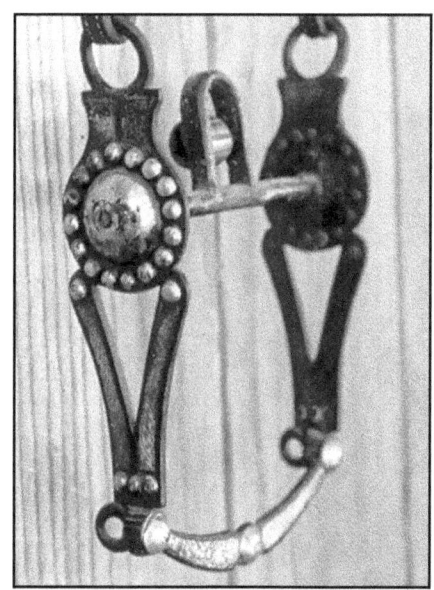

20. Unusual Half Breed-type mouthpiece with Sonora cheek – This is a leverage bit. I have never seen one just like this. The smooth front of the port should give a soft feel to the palate. My first thoughts would be for a medium-to-thick-tongued horse because of the width and height of the port. I would like to try this bit some day.

21. Modified Half-Breed mouthpiece center-hung with a modified Las Cruces type (The Cross) cheek – This is a leverage bit that is very fast and will give a lot of feel back into your hand. Being center-hung, it will start to compress the tongue faster than a mouthpiece that is forward-hung.

Bridle Bits, cont.

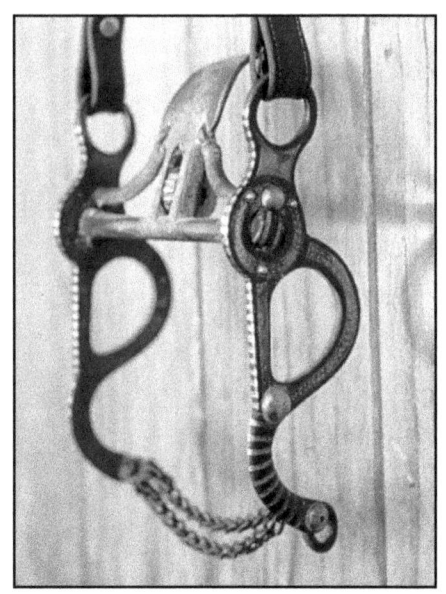

22. Big Spoon Spade that is center-hung with modified Santa Paula cheeks – This can be a signal bit or a leverage bit and will start to compress the tongue faster than a forward-hung mouthpiece.

23. San Joaquin mouthpiece with hood and Big Santa Barbara cheeks – This is a leverage bit that will give a lot of feel back into your hand.

24. Modified Half Breed with Big Santa Barbara cheeks – This is a leverage bit that gives good feel back into your hand.

25. Traditional high port Frog mouthpiece with Big Santa Barbara cheeks – This operates as a signal bit or a leverage bit. Either way, it gives a lot of feel back into your hand.

26. Open Spoon Spade mouthpiece with lots of rollers for the tongue to play with, and Fiesta style cheeks – This can be a signal bit or a leverage bit. Mobilization of the tongue is a factor in helping to keep the jaw muscles relaxed. It is very important that the poll and jaw remain relaxed through the whole training processes. The purpose of braces seen in this bit and other bits that have brace bars is to pick up some additional feel from the curve groove of the lips, which on most horses, is a sensitive area. These braces are usually found only on bits that are high enough to signal. When using a signal bit we generally set it higher into the curve groove of the lips than we would the leverage bit. The leverage bit being set slightly lower so the horse can pick it up where it feels the best.

I want to thank Jack Bassett, owner of D BAR M Western Store in Reno, Nevada, for the use of some of these bits for this book.

~ Mike Bridges

Chapter 12
Is My Horse Ready for the Bridling Process?

You can start a horse in the bridling process at any stage of his training. This is not retraining a horse. It is introducing a new signal form for him to respond to for things that he already knows how to do.

I've started two horses right after their first few rides immediately into the two-rein. The first one in the late 1960s and the second one was in the early 1970s. Both went through all the training steps using the two-reining process of a two-rein bosal along with a bridle bit.

Both horses turned out pretty mediocre. They could do the cattle work (gathering, separating and the roping). They got the job done but from the beginning and at the end of the training process they both ended up with quite a bit of brace through different parts of their bodies. They weren't quite as relaxed as my other horses when asked to frame their bodies and work with speed.

I believe that these negative things, the bracing and slight mental stress which ended up in these two horses, was caused by too fast of a hand signal from the two-rein bosal. There is no way to make a slow signal with the bosal tight to the face of the horse when it is under the bridle headstall. When a horse is trying to respond to a fast signal and does not have the ability developed to re-balance himself with that much speed, he will brace different parts of his body in order to get through the movement.

Little corrections that have to be made with the hands are very fast and, at times, too fast, and can exacerbate the problems.

Both of these horses had soft personalities and were not spooky. I picked them for that reason. I think that if I had picked horses with strong personalities (sometimes referred to as "hot" horses), the end result of this little experiment would have turned out with even poorer results. Everything is happening too fast in the early training and little mistakes made with the hands turn into big mistakes with the speed of the signals. During my twenties, in the 1960s, I just *knew* that the process of building one of these bridle horses could be made to happen faster. I experimented with the hackamore and two-rein to shorten the time before and during the bridling, and I screwed up my fair share of horses. I didn't ruin them but I didn't bring out their full potential. The old timers were right and confirmed what I had already been taught but had not taken to heart: you need patience and must build this horse one step at a time if your goal is to end up with a great horse, ridden one-handed in a bridle bit with balance, and without body braces or mental stress.

In time, you will get to a point where you will know if your horse is ready for the bridling process. Some of the questions you should ask yourself before you start, and be able to answer in the affirmative, are:

1. Is his ability to balance and re-balance at the level I would like it to be, whether he is on diagonal balance or arc balance?

2. Are his transitions up or down in gait smooth and fluid?

3. Are canter departs fluid and within the stride asked, both sides and directions?

4. Can he handle changes of speed within the gait, speeding it up, slowing it down?

5. Can he maintain a frame that requires his back to be open for a period of time?

6. Will he come back from a passive rein into my hand without resistance while driving his hips forward?

7. Does he have understanding of the indirect rein from my single hand work in the hackamore?

8. Does the back-up have the distance I want with fluidness?

9. Are my turnarounds at the level I want?

10. Is my help for the horse in the cow work coming mostly from my body signals now?

If I answered any of these questions with a "no," I would do some more work to get the weak areas improved before moving on to the two-rein. I'm not in a hurry to get him into the bridle. He has his whole life ahead of him. When I do get there, I want him to be as good or better than he was when riding him in two hands.

Bill Berner with a nice frame on a two-rein horse.

Chapter 13
STARTING THE HORSE IN THE TWO-REIN

USING WHAT YOU HAVE

When I was a kid and young man, most of the horsemen I was around started their horses in the two-rein process with the bridle bit they were going to end with. If they wanted a spade bit horse, that was the bridle bit used from the start of the process.

The spade bit could be used as a leverage bit or as a signal bit, depending on the horse's training to this point and the desire of the rider. If the person wanted just a leverage bit bridle horse, he would use a lower port bit through the bridling process and continued with it when the horse was straight-up in the bridle.

Whatever direction you decided to go with this horse—signal, leverage, or a combination of both—you worked to pick a bit that fit the horse's mouth and mental make-up.

Most young buckaroos didn't own a lot of bridle bits. Buckarooing is not an occupation that pays very much money. If I had only one or two bridle bits, that is what I used and I could get the bridling done and finish with a nice bridle horse. However, that particular horse might not have as "bright a mouth" and give as much feel back to my hands if the bar and port of the bridle bit didn't quite fit his mouth.

The cattle business is a small, closed society and the men and women who make a living horseback in it tend to make lasting friendships and partner up with others who have similar desires regarding their horsemanship and cowmanship skills. In these friendships, bridle bits are lent back and forth in an effort to find the best bridle bit for a given horse. Oftentimes, it was the older guys whom you would borrow from because they had more bits to choose from. This gave me the opportunity to try different mouth and cheek pieces on different horses.

As the years went by, I acquired more variety in bridle bits and I became one of the older guys lending bits out to younger buckaroos who couldn't buy one just to try.

Long passive rein with a three-finger spread. The hackamore rein is slightly drawing the horse to the left.

Experimentation with Bits

Through these years of trying different bridle bits, and finally getting to a point where I owned a small variety of mouthpieces from low port to high port bits, I discovered an interesting fact in the process of building a spade bit bridle horse.

If I started the two-rein process with a low port leverage bit that fit the mouth well, I could develop mental confidence in the horse much quicker than starting with the spade bit or one of the higher port bits. There was less weight for him to support and less change in configuration of his tongue.

The trade-off is that these lower port bits give very little feel back into your hands. However, I'm willing to give that up at the start to get this quicker mental and physical confidence.

As this confidence builds through the work, I will move up in bridle mouthpiece to one that will create more feel in the horse's mouth and back to my hands. After two or three changes, I will move up to the spade bit and develop understanding with the horse to find and respond to the signal.

The signal consists of the top of the spade lifting off of the tongue and not touching soft tissue or, if he misses that one, then when it touches the hard palate before it comes to leverage at the jawbone of the horse through the chin strap.

My goal with each horse is to make a signal bit horse. They are the fastest to your hands and require the least movement of your hands. For most horses, the spade bit is the fastest because it sits high enough in the mouth where there is room between the tongue and the hard palate.

When activated, there is space enough to be free of soft tissue before touching the hard palate. Other ports that are high enough to signal must be at least high enough to reach that part of the mouth where the hard palate starts lifting away from the tongue.

When the bit is activated by the rider's hand, the top of the port leaves the surface of the tongue and then immediately touches the hard palate. The signal is the change from one surface to the other before the leverage takes place. In the lower port bits, they are far enough down in the horse's mouth that the tongue and hard palate are together encasing the mouthpiece in soft tissue and allowing the port to move into each surface but not change from one to the other. That way, there's no chance for a signal. They operate by leverage through the chinstrap at the jawbone of the horse.

Bill Berner with his horse in his hand making a turn back to the right with the cow. The horse is over his hocks and on the inside pivot foot.

CREATING LEVERAGE WITH THE CHINSTRAP

There is a difference in how to set the chinstrap for a leverage bit or a signal bit. For the leverage bit, I will set the chinstrap so I can get just one finger or a finger-and-a-half inserted sideways not flat, between the jawbone of the horse and the chinstrap with the slack taken out. I have small hands and thin fingers.

If the chinstrap is too tight, I won't have enough release. If the chinstrap is too loose, the port of the bit will turn too much into the hard palate, prying the mouth open. Jawbone shape from one horse to the next can vary quite a bit. If I use that bit on another horse, I will reset my chinstrap.

Chinstraps used in this discipline should be made from some type of soft, pliable leather. I prefer a chinstrip made out of harness leather or latigo leather that has two buckles for adjustments. If you're showing your horse, in some instances, you may have to use a chinstrap with only one buckle. You don't have to have buckles but they make the adjustments much easier.

For the signal bit, I will set the chinstrap so I can get one-and-a-half-to-two fingers, inserted sideways not flat, and with the slack taken out between the jawbone of the horse and the chinstrap so that the upper part of the port can move off the tongue before leverage takes place.

My two-reining process, which usually takes one-to-two years, has evolved to a point where I now have five favorite bits: A MAC (Guitron Frog) with a Hash-Knife cheek; a Hill Frog (formal name unknown) with standard Santa Barbara cheeks; an El Gato Frog with Big Santa Barbara cheeks; a San Joaquin with an uncovered port and the port built as high as the hanger holes with Big Santa Barbara cheeks; and my Al Tietjen (maker) Spanish-style spade bits.

These bridle bits cover my early work in the two-rein, the middle work and my finish work. Among them, I can fit the different shaped palates I run into. Not that I don't use other bits, too, because I do. This particular set of bits gives great feel back into my hand, except for the MAC Guitron Frog. It is like the rest of the low port bits; almost no feel or very little. However, this particular mouthpiece is very easy for a horse to pick up and support as I am starting to build mental confidence. I've hung it on a lot of horses in the United States and Europe, and even a few with injured tongues and as of yet I have not found a horse that won't pick it up with his tongue and hold it with confidence.

That is what I use it for, as a confidence builder. As soon as I feel he has good confidence, I will move up to more port so I can get more feel back into my hand.

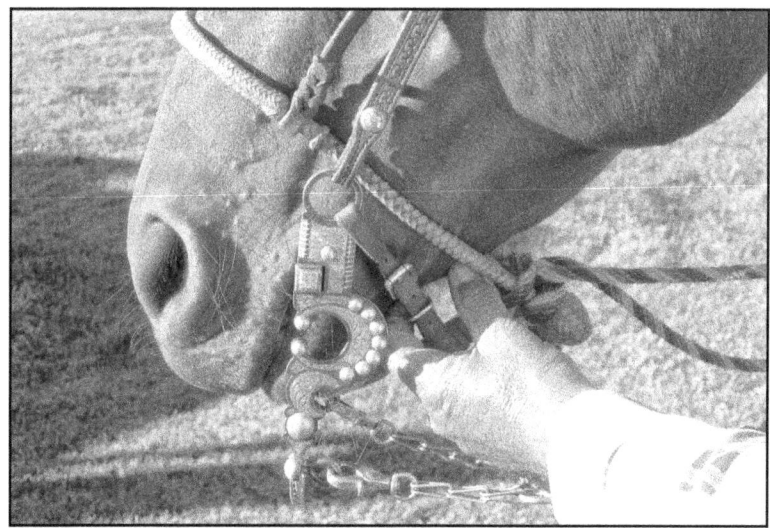
Checking the chinstrap.

The Romal Reins

The bridle reins used in this discipline are traditionally braided rawhide and are made one continuous length. They can vary from six-to-eight feet in length. The reins that attach to the bridle bit are connected with a leather thong to another braided single rein called the romal. The purpose of the romal is to act like a counter-weight, so that when you put the reins in your hand they will stay put without a lot of hand pressure, neither sliding forward or backward.

The diameter of the bridle reins and the romal when they are made, and the length, is entirely a personal preference of the rider. They can be anywhere from a quarter of an inch to a half-inch in size, depending on what you prefer. I, personally, prefer a small rein with lots of buttons because I have small hands.

There are usually braided buttons around the reins and romal. Their purpose is to add weight and to help keep the sweat of the horse from getting onto the main rein. They also work as a friction buffer as the rein moves against the neck. It is much easier to replace a button that has worn out through use than to build a whole new rein.

Putting it On

Now, I've picked the bit I want to begin with and fitted the two-rein bosal to the horse's face. I will leave the "whooie" knot loose as I bridle the horse with the bit. This is a new experience for him and I want to be smooth in my presentation of the bridle bit into the horse's mouth. I will leave one side of the chinstrap undone as I place the bit in his mouth and remove it from his mouth. On most horses, I will put the bridle bit into their mouths two-to-four times without the bosal on their face so that it is easier for them to open their mouths.

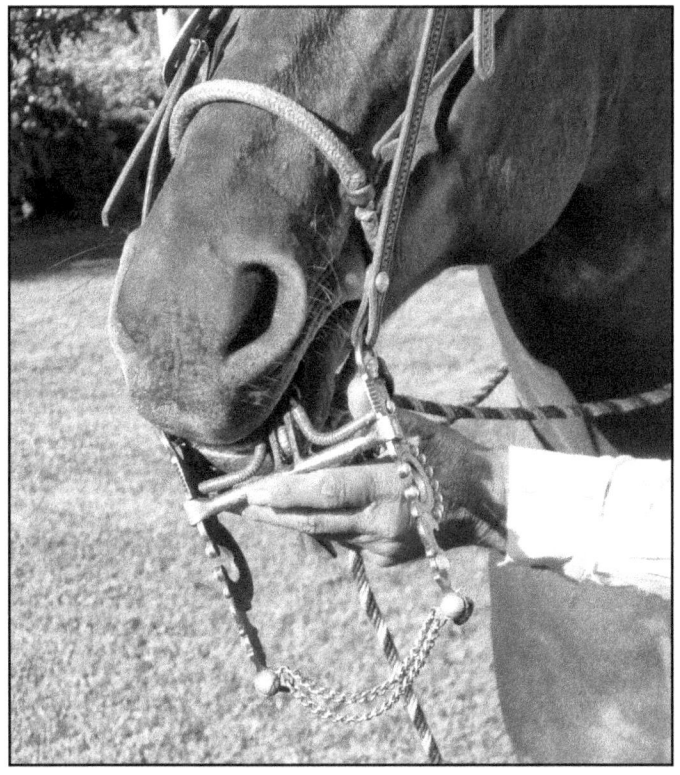

Bridling the horse for the first time with the two-rein bosal around his face can be a little difficult for the horse mentally so be patient and help him with your fingers by massaging the tongue, gums or the hard palate.

After the bridle bit is in the horse's mouth, I set the chin strap for that horse and then tighten the "whooie" knot on the bosal to bring the bars of the bosal in close enough to influence the lower lip muscles of the horse. I place the bridle reins over the neck of the horse so that they are on his neck between the saddle horn and his ears and place the bosal reins so that they are between the bridle reins and the ears of the horse.

I'm going to hold both sets of reins in one hand, but I want the bosal reins to be the primary signaling rein and the bridle reins are going to be secondary for quite a while.

This is a big mental transition for the horse to read more and more of the hand signal from the indirect rein. My previous single handwork will help. But now the signals are going to get very fast. Until I see good understanding by the horse, I want to stay out of his mouth as far as indirect rein influence. I will use the bridle reins to help support the bit and to check him off into my hand standing still, and also while he is moving forward some of the time as we are doing our work.

Hand Influences on the Reins

Checking off while moving forward.

Your hand influence to the bridle reins is now limited to a relatively small area in this one hand position. I call this area the "bridle box." It is important not to move your hand outside of the box for a hand signal.

If you do need to do more with your hand than can be accomplished inside the bridle box, you can put your bridle rein around your saddle horn and tuck the romal under your leg so the reins don't bounce around. You can then use two hands on the bosal rein and take the hand influence outside the bridle box to help fix whatever problem you are addressing.

You will run into this occasionally when there is a lack of understanding mentally by the horse or when he is testing your program. This should be a short fix, maybe five minutes, and then it's back to one hand. If this is a bigger problem, something you missed, quit the two-reining and go back to the hackamore to fix it.

Over time, each rider develops his or her own style of how to use their hands to influence the bridle reins and the two-rein. Your goal is to be able to have less direct rein influence and more indirect rein influence as time goes on without bracing by your horse. You are going to have to move your fingers around the reins so that you can move the two-rein more toward the top of your hand or from there to the bottom of your hand. This is how you manage the reins to have more or less indirect rein influence.

When you move your hand for a signal and you don't quite have the right spread in your fingers between the bosal reins, you can reach with your romal hand to the top of the bosal rein and shorten the side you need for more influence. Most of the time when I need to do this, it is the direct rein that needs to be shortened. It happens when I don't have the right spread in my fingers between the bosal reins for this movement at this moment for the horse. I need to keep doing the work and keep asking for more understanding of the indirect rein.

This is an easy fix during the movement to help the horse understand. As soon as this correction is understood, I let the rein slide through my fingers to its original position.

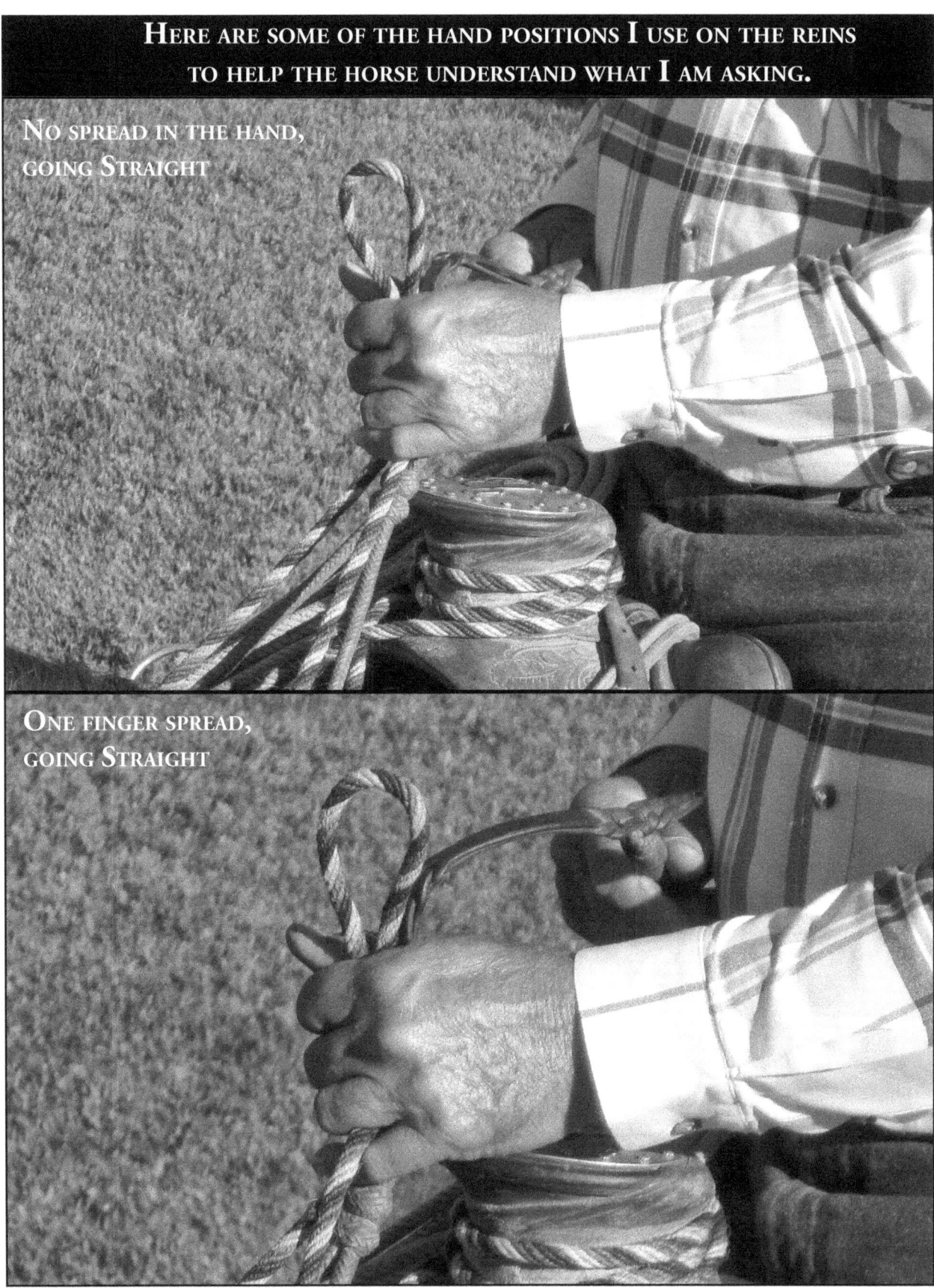

Here are some of the hand positions I use on the reins to help the horse understand what I am asking.

No spread in the hand, going Straight

One finger spread, going Straight

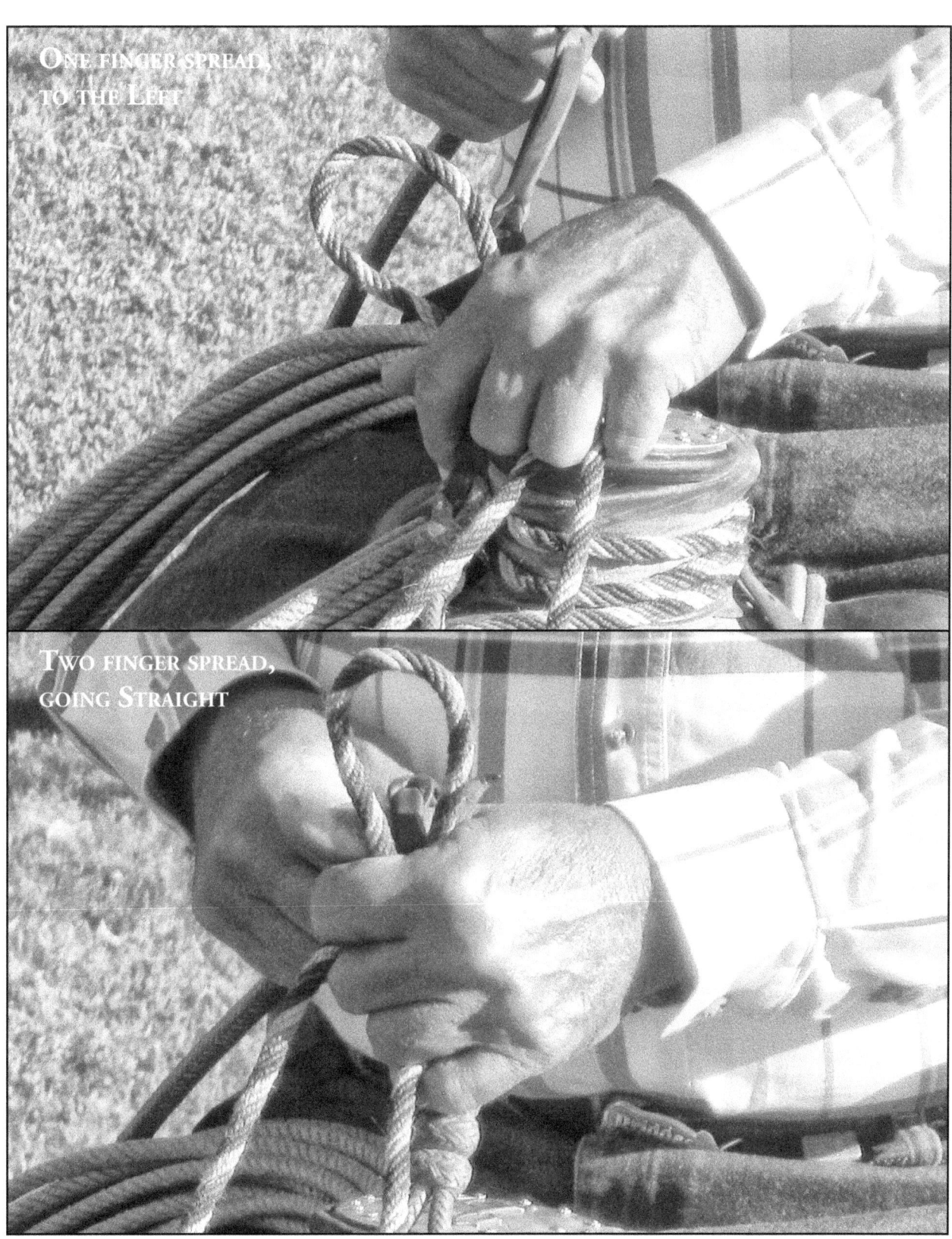

Chapter 13   *Starting the Horse in the Two-Rein*

Hand Positions, cont.

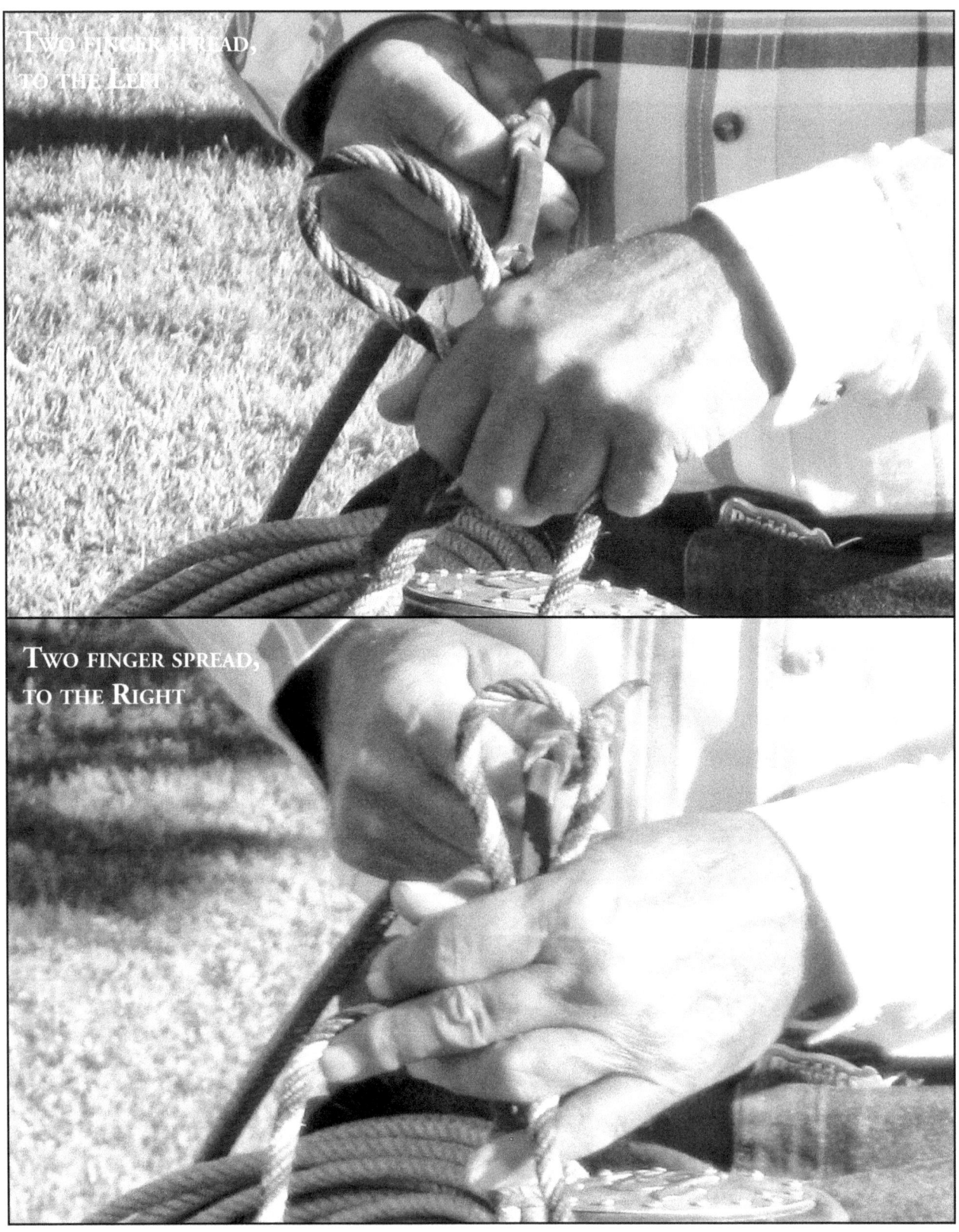

Two finger spread, to the Left

Two finger spread, to the Right

Hand Positions, cont.

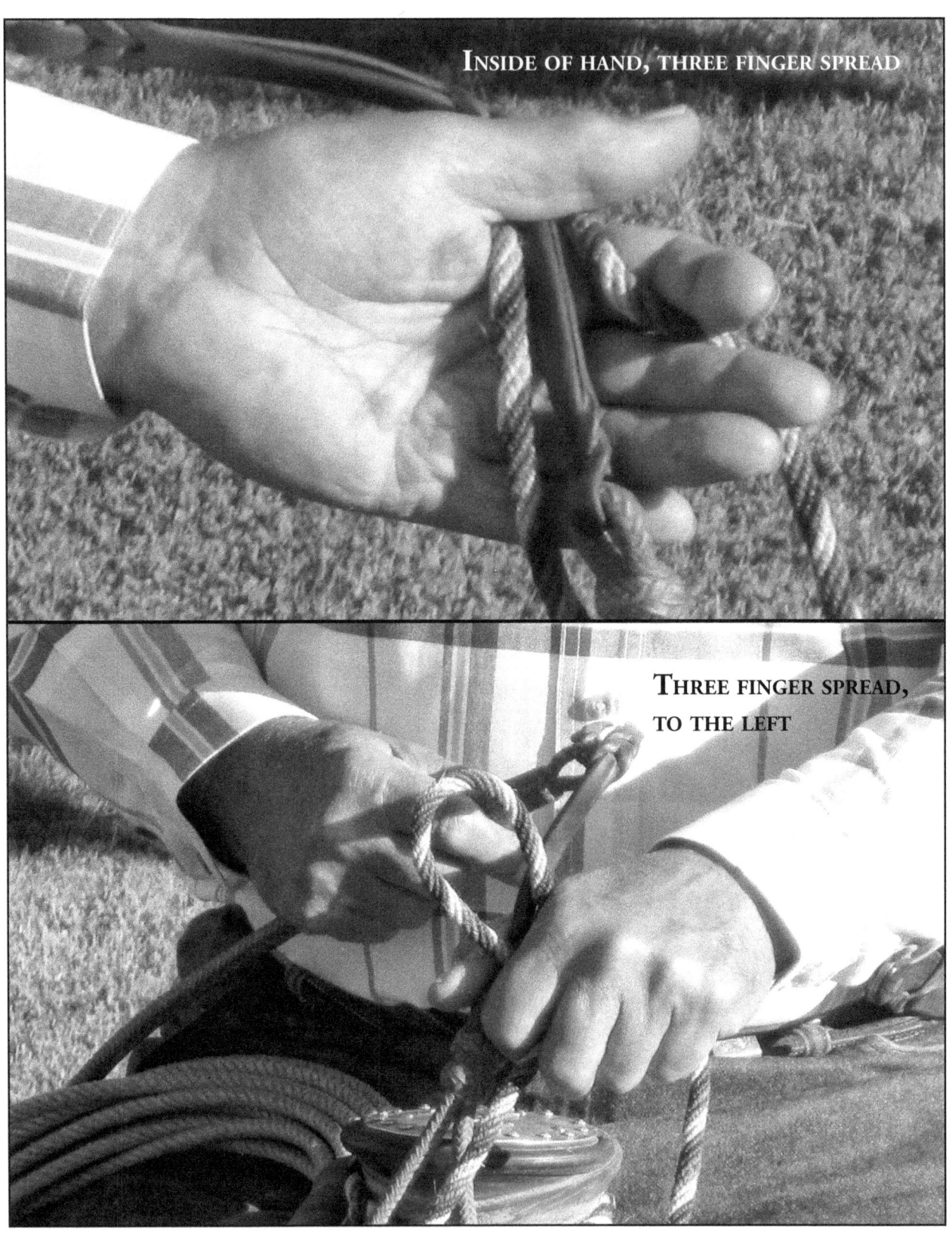

Inside of hand, three finger spread

Three finger spread, to the left

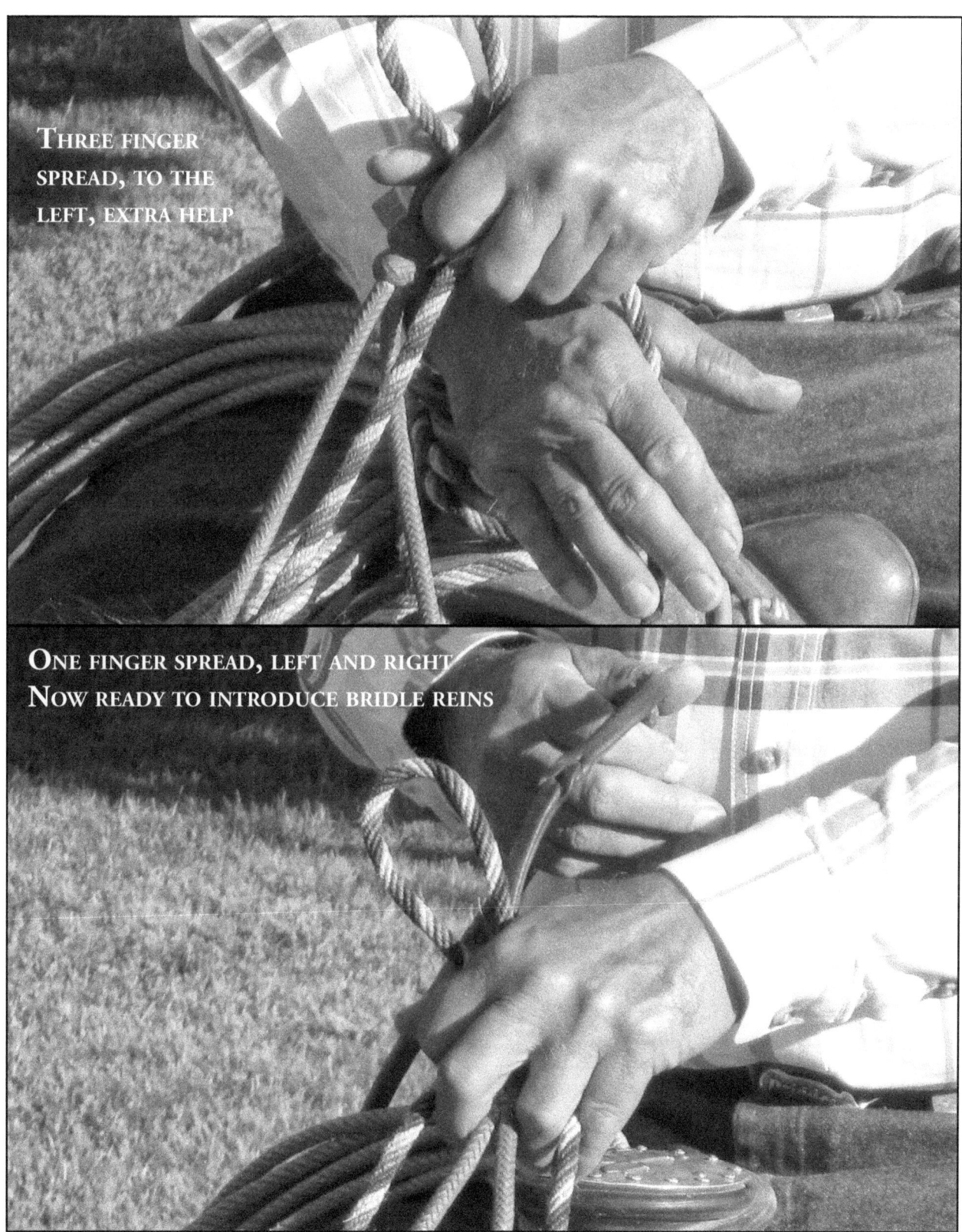

Hand Positions, cont.

INSIDE OF HAND, TWO REIN IN SUPPORT POSITION, BRIDLE REIN IS NOW PRIMARY REIN

Signs of Progress to Look For

After a few months of two-reining the horse, the hand signals are being read by the horse from the bosal. The bridle reins are in a support position to keep the bridle bit from rattling around in his mouth as he makes transition from movement to movement.

You will get to a point where there is less spread in your fingers between the bosal reins. The horse is reading and understanding the indirect rein with very little direct rein influence. That means it's now time to start bringing the bridle reins into play along with the bosal reins. You still keep the bosal reins ahead of the bridle reins, but will now shorten the length of the bridle reins in your hand so that when you move your hand the bridle reins makes direct contact with the bit along with contact to the neck of the horse.

Your bosal reins can be the first signal before the bridle reins if they are shorter in your hand than the bridle reins. You can make bridle-rein influence from very little or to all bridle reins depending on rein management between your two-rein and your bridle rein.

This is how I know my horse is at a stage where he has complete confidence with his mouth through all transitions and movements and full understanding of indirect rein influence along with direct reins for the frame in the stop and the back-up. I am now ready to start riding him straight in the bridle.

Bill Berner positioning for a cut on the red yearling.

The inside of my hand with a long passive rein (mail box rein) with a three-finger spread.

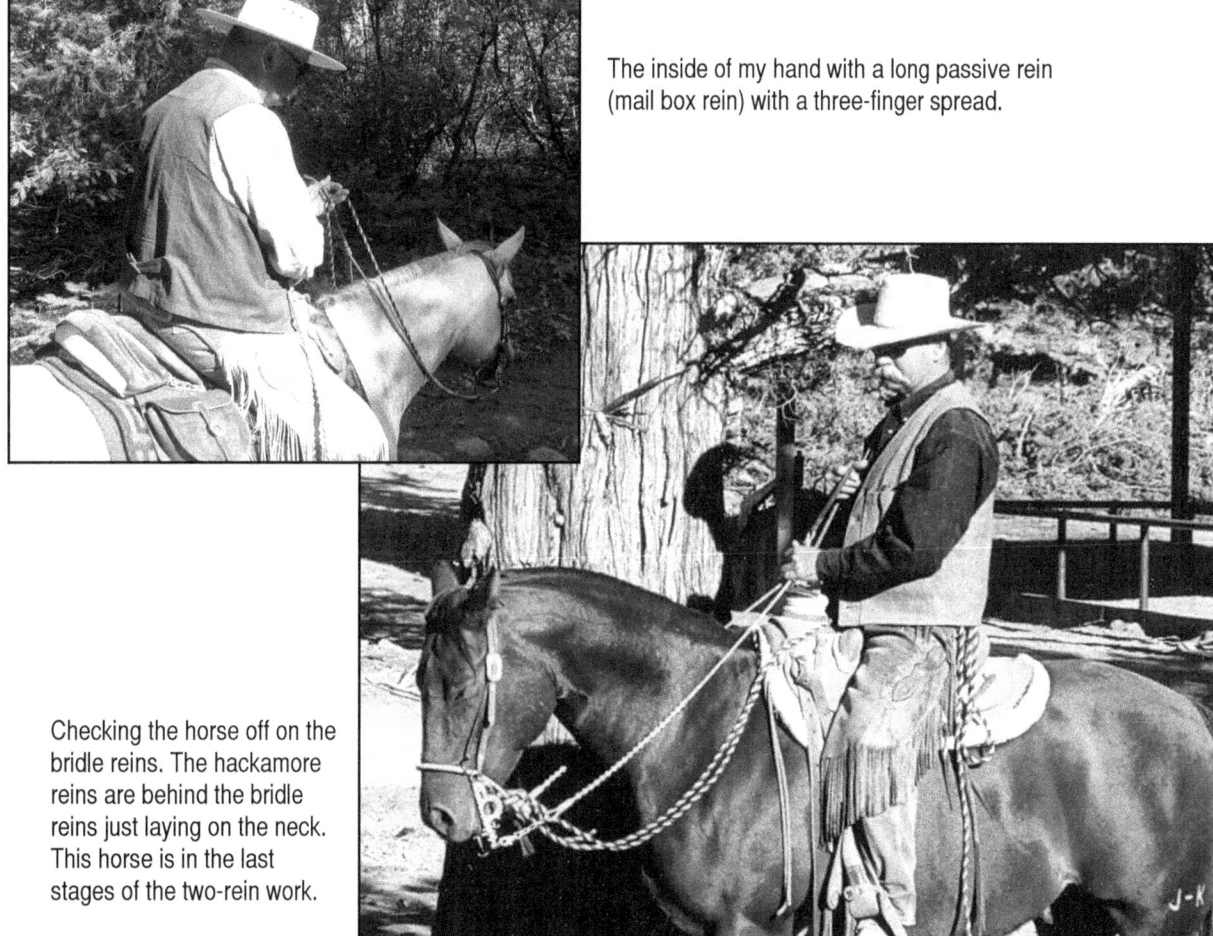

Checking the horse off on the bridle reins. The hackamore reins are behind the bridle reins just laying on the neck. This horse is in the last stages of the two-rein work.

Chapter 14
RIDING THE HORSE STRAIGHT IN THE BRIDLE

At the very end of the two-rein work, I'm using the bridle reins equally with the bosal reins.

If the movement is passive and I don't have contact with the mouth, the action of the bridle rein and bosal rein influence is just to the neck of the horse. If the movement requires frame on the horse, I bring him back into my hand with both sets of reins. Simultaneously, the bridle rein asks for response through the mouth and bosal reins asks by a slight rotation of the nose button. With that, I can then do the movement or movements I need to get the work done.

Bill English setting up the cut on the red yearling with his horse in his hand.

At some point, I will decide that my horse is ready to be ridden straight in the bridle. That decision develops over a period of rides or can come all of a sudden while doing some intense work.

I had a mare that was a very difficult horse to train but was also a very talented athlete. She was not afraid of anything, had a very strong personality, continually tested the program and could get on the muscle for long periods of time. She was also bad to be around on the ground and would sometimes kick at your feet when you were riding. Needless to say, she was not the most favorite of horses I owned. There were days I could have shot her and packed my saddle back to camp if I had had a gun with me. This kind of nonsense went on for the first three-and-a-half years of the training process.

The first block on the yearling after the cut was made. The energy in the horse's body is already going left. Bill's leg is opening the door for the move.

Then, late one morning, while gathering cattle. I was side-hilling around a knob on some pretty steep ground and I felt her melt underneath me. From that day on, she never got on the muscle again. Her test of the program became very slight on the ground and while being ridden. I showed this mare some and she did really well. Just before the last time I showed her, a fellow bought her from me with the understanding that I could show her this last time and we would split the money and I could keep the merchandise. This mare won the event and at the award ceremony he asked me if I would put this mare in the bridle for him. We made a deal and I rode this mare for two more years, putting her into the bridle.

At about a year and eight months into the two-reining of this mare, one morning I was splitting cows from calves in the gate. I did two bunches and at the start of the third bunch, I dropped the two-rein and went straight off the bridle rein. She was ready and I could feel it in her body. I've had a few others that this has happened with. It is a defining moment and you know when it's there.

Horses I've Bridled

At this stage of my life, I have bridled or have done some bridling work on about 100 horses. Most of the time, it does not happen as a defining moment but develops over a period of a few rides at some point during the two-reining.

When I do go to riding the horse straight off the bridle, I don't abandon the two rein right away. I move the bosal reins behind the bridle reins so that the bridle reins are first and are now the primary rein, and the bosal rein is secondary, coming into play after the bridle has made movement in the mouth of the horse. I think of the bosal and its rein as a safety net if I get into a little trouble.

Roy Bridges on Mud, a very nice Spade Bit Bridle horse.

I usually ride this way for three-to-four months. Gradually, I will let the bosal rein get longer and longer in my hand until I reach a point where I just hang it over my thumb or wrist and the only influence it has is the slight movement against the neck of the horse. This safety net concept of the bosal and its rein, when I have reached this stage of training on most horses, is really more of a mental comfort for me than a necessity.

On a few horses, it can be of great help for a quick moment of stabilization or correction without overpowering the mouth of the horse. Usually four months after riding with just the bridle bit, the horse's confidence level will be high enough that he can handle a pull on the reins to help support him if he slips or stumbles or I need to make a small correction through the mouth.

Jim Reilly riding straight off the bridle with the hackamore rein over his wrist as a safety net. The hackamore rein is behind the bridle rein. If it was to be picked up and used, it would be the secondary rein. The bridle rein would come into play first.

Odd Things Happen

About 30 years ago, one of the horses I owned was ready to start in the bridling process. He was eight years old, very brave and things just didn't rattle him. I had a little more than five years work on him and most of that work was riding in the snaffle bit. He had very thin curve grooves in his lips, which is good for a snaffle bit horse. He was very bright in the mouth and gave that velvet feeling back into my hands. His movements and balance were where I wanted them and I was really looking forward to bridling him. His tongue was on the average-to-thick side and his hard palate was shaped like a culvert or the top of a pipe.

When I first put the bridle bit in his mouth—a Salinas mouthpiece with Santa Paula cheek—he dropped his face to vertical and lowered his poll below his withers. Occasionally, you will see this on some horses, especially if they are real light in the mouth. The bridle bit weighs considerably more than a snaffle bit and requires the tongue to configure itself differently than with snaffle bit.

If this happens, with most horses after a minute or two the horse will try to pick up the bit with his tongue and will raise his poll back up to a more normal position. This horse didn't do that. He just stayed in this negative position. I unbridled him and rebridled him and the same thing happened. I did this a couple of times and the results were the same. I quit trying and unbridled him, put him in the snaffle bit and went about my work with the idea that I would try again when I got back in the afternoon. The ride turned out to be longer than expected and I didn't get in until after dark.

The next time I tried the bridle bit was on his next turn after two days of rest. I waited until after the ride when I got back to camp. The same thing happened. He fell to vertical and dropped his poll as soon as the bridle bit was in his mouth. I thought I would lead him around to put some motion in his body to help him get out of this negative position.

With the halter around his neck and no reins on the bridle bit, I led him off. At first he went past the vertical and dropped his poll farther down. His body was tight and his expression showed great mental stress. I kept leading him forward. After about 20 yards, his poll started to come up. After a few more yards the poll was in a normal position but his body was very tight. I stopped there, scratched him some and unbridled him. I made a fuss over him some more, then re-bridled and started back to my tack room. He went to the negative position, but came out of it quicker than the first time. When I got to the tack room, I quit for the day.

This brave horse that didn't spook at anything and could lay right against cows was scared to death of this bridle bit. I had a big hurdle to get over with this horse. I started to pony him with a bridle bit without reins once or twice a week.

Over a period of a couple of months, he became comfortable packing it and his body relaxed. I switched from leading him with the halter to using a two-rein bosal. The day came when I thought he was ready to ride in the two-rein. But before I got on him, I wanted to check him off with the bridle reins in my hand. Standing next to him, I shortened the bridle reins and he immediately went past the vertical.

When I raised my hand to raise his poll back up, he threw his head up in the air. Things were not looking good here. I had never had, nor seen, a schooled horse this scared of a bridle bit.

I kept on ponying this horse with a bridle bit in his mouth and also added the bridle reins, but not short enough for contact with the mouth. I left the bridle reins long enough to swing a little bit with the motion of his body so he would think a little about supporting the bridle bit with his tongue. Every once in a while I would stop, reach over and get his bridle reins in my hand and shorten them until I could just feel the bit and then close my hand on the rein but not move it. I didn't do this everyday but a couple of times a week. It took a couple more months before the start of the riding. I also tried some different bridle bits and ended up using the Guitron Frog with a Hashknife cheek. The rest of the process went forward in good shape. The introduction to more bridle bits with higher ports was not a big deal to him, and when he got over his fear, it was gone.

When I got to the point of riding him more off the bridle rein than the bosal rein, his mouth was very quiet and very light but I could see that when I needed to help stabilize him with the bridle rein, he would lose a slight bit of confidence.

With this horse, I used the two-rein bosal and reins as a safety net for a long time after he was being ridden off the bridle bit. It took about seven months of riding off the bridle reins before he gained complete confidence.

A friend of mine now has this horse and he is still going strong, and is everything he should be. This was the toughest horse to start into the two-rein I have ever dealt with. It took longer when just on the bridle reins to gain that last element of complete confidence but it was worth it. He turned out to be a very nice horse and it was quite a learning experience for me as well.

Roy Bridges dragging a calf to the fire, horse is straight in the bridle.

Setting up the cut straight in the bridle on a loose rein.

How to Hold the Reins

When you are riding straight off the bridle reins, one hand on the reins and the other hand holding the romal, both hands need to always be relaxed but not dead. They need to have life in them. That does not mean a lot of movement. You are limited to the size of the imaginary bridle box and must keep your hand inside that area so you don't tilt the bit in the horse's mouth.

If I am riding my horse forward on a passive rein most of the time, the rein is just hanging from my thumb by the strap that connects the reins to the romal. If I shorten the rein with my romal hand to make contact with the horse's mouth to do a movement, I'll leave my hand pretty open and have some spread in the fingers but in a cupped position on the reins.

Never thread your fingers between the bridle reins. Let me repeat: never thread your fingers between the bridle reins. That will tilt the bit in the horse's mouth and the horse will start to brace the other way from the direction you are asking him to go.

The movement I have asked for is easy and I don't need a lot of energy going down the reins. As I bring the horse more into my hand to ask for more topline frame, I close my hand around the reins more but never real tight. I will use the tension in my hand and each finger, adding and subtracting energy to tell the horse how much I want out of that signal.

Horses are very perceptive to this change in energy on the rein and can read it in their mouths. I need good control of all parts of my hand, including the back of my hand and each finger so I can change the amount of power in my hand from the bottom to the top, one finger at a time. I also need to be able to soften the back of my hand when fingers are closed around the reins.

In passive rein positions, where there is no direct contact with the mouth of the horse, my hand signals are almost casual. Most of the time they are activated from the strap between the rein and the romal.

A nice right shoulder-in straight in the bridle. Kitty Gratzer is the rider.

If I wanted to ask the horse to go left, I would move my hand up and to the left, bringing the right rein against the horse's neck; not hard into the neck, but with a brushing action. The upward movement of the hand slightly left slows down the left hind leg; the right rein brushing the neck moves the shoulder. I remember to keep my hand inside the width of the bridle box. If I ask to go right, everything would be just the opposite. It goes without saying that I am also using my other body signals that I've developed with these hand signals.

In the stop, I move my hand up and back just enough to feel the bit. I refer to it as being at the end of the rein but not influencing the face. In backing up with this passive rein and no frame on the horse, the signals for the back up come from my body. The rein position

The horse is straight in the bridle, starting to stop as the cow yields. This shows a nice working frame on the horse for this position.

again is to move my hand up enough to be at the end of the rein, then no movement of the hand. If I need to help him continue, I will move the hand up and back more to create direct contact with the mouth. As soon as I feel the start of movement backwards, I release the contact and just be at the end of the rein.

We spend a lot of time riding on a passive rein. There can be hours of time doing my job that does not require me to make a move with a collected rein and frame on my horse. These passive moves don't require me to telegraph a lot of energy down the rein. The hand can be very open and casual in its effect.

The California style of holding the reins is with the knuckles of the hand facing toward the ears of the horse and the thumb being the highest part of the hand. The Mexican style is with the palm of the hand facing up and the knuckles of the hand facing down toward the mane line of the neck. I use the Mexican style sometimes when riding along with a passive rein. It is a comfortable change for me when not much is going on.

When the movements I am going to ask the horse to do require some degree of collection of his body, from a little to a whole lot, my hand influence on the reins becomes more critical. I am using my whole body to communicate with the horse to indicate what direction I will go, how fast we will get there and what frame will be on the horse before, during and after I get there.

My hand is part of that influence and can develop to where I can have little conversations with my horse through the reins as things are happening during movements if the horse is in a degree of collection. These little conversations can consist of tightening one or two fingers more or less than the rest of the hand, more softness in the back of the hand, changing the cant of the hand in or out or back. The horse will read them through the energy change in the rein. If my other work was good before I got to this point, my horse will recognize the change in energy and respond to it.

If I am doing work that requires frame on my horse, I need to bring him back into my hand. I can accomplish this two different ways. First, by using my romal hand, lifting the reins and pulling them through my rein hand until I'm at the length I want. Or I can do it by holding the top of the romal where the strap attaches and then sliding my rein hand down the rein until I'm where I want to be.

Once the horse is in my hand, the action of the hand to deliver signals needs to become very limited in its movements side-to-side and forward and backward. It's more like a joystick staying more in one spot. The different angles of the hand and the tension in the hand, along with individual fingers, is what conveys the message to the horse.

If I had my horse in my hand or if I was just at the end of the rein and I wanted more face on the horse for more nuchal ligament influence to the withers, I would just move the bottom of my hand toward my saddle horn. This shortens the rein equally, activating the port of the bit in the horse's mouth. As the horse comes into my hand, I bring my hand back to its normal position, holding the horse's face with the power in my bottom two fingers.

If I was to ask the horse to flex to the left from this position, I would move the bottom of my rein hand in and toward his right scapula, staying centered over the neck.

If I was going to execute a left turn, I would hold the cant in the lower part of my hand to hold the flexion and move my rein hand slightly to the left from center of the mane line to bring the right rein against the neck of the horse.

If I wanted that turn to be over the left pivot foot, I would put backward motion in the rein hand as I moved it to the left. If I was going to create this to the right, everything would be reversed.

In the stop and back up, my rein hand needs to stay centered over the mane line. The length of my reins, the cant of the bottom of my hand and the amount of power expressed by my hand will determine how much face is on the horse as I execute the movements.

If I am at the end of the rein and the knuckle of my pinky finger is more toward the ears of the horse than my index finger knuckle, I will have very little face influence. After my hand has reached vertical back toward the saddle horn, the more I move the little knuckle down, the more the horse's face moves toward the vertical.

I have to keep my hand quiet and soft, with no quick or hard movements. It's important to develop control of the power in all parts of the hand. I work to send signals to the mouth very subtly and, after the signal has been answered, enhance that movement by slight nuances using the expression of power in my hand, adding or subtracting while still holding the signal.

This all should be happening with ounces of pressure with a signal bit and no more than three pounds of pressure in the leverage bits. When I talk about three pounds of pressure, I am referring to the amount of pressure it would take to release the trigger on a gun that was set for a three-pound break off. That is not very much movement or pressure.

BEING STRAIGHT UP IN THE BRIDLE

When you get to the point that your horse has total confidence being ridden off the bridle reins and you know that the two-rein bosal is no longer needed as a safety net and you remove it, your horse is now straight up in the bridle. After you have done away with the two-rein, which was also your get-down rope to lead your horse, you need to add a neck rope to the horse so you still have a way to lead him, without using the bridle reins.

Leading a horse by the bridle reins with a bridle bit in his mouth will dull the mouth over time because the horse cannot support the bit with his tongue when you pull the reins forward. You have spent years putting this all together; use a get-down to lead your bridle horse!

The get-down rope can be attached to the horse in different ways. How is a matter of personal choice. One way is not more or less correct than any other. It is just style.

I like a get-down rope 5/16 inch in size and very soft. You can tie the rope around the neck of the horse at the throatlatch with a knot that won't slip, and then bring the rope back to the saddle or to your chap belt. Or you can take it through a bridle bosal (a very small, soft round or oblong bosal that goes around the face of the horse under the bridle headstall) and then back to the saddle.

An alternative is to just attach it to the bridle bosal, then back to the saddle or chap belt. Often the old-timers would tie the get-down rope around the base of the neck using a fancy Alamar knot if they knew they were not going to get down much during the day.

Some riders didn't want a bridle bosal on their horse's face. They wanted to show that their horse's mouth was very quiet and would not open during the work without anything other than the bridle and headstall on the head of the horse that might have influence.

You will develop your own style, the more bridle horses you ride and train. However, your style is not as important as what your horse can do!

Chapter 15

POLISHING THE STONE

I don't believe I've ever finished a horse to the point where there was no more room for improvement.

I've ridden a lot of horses through their eighteenth or nineteenth year, having them take a regular turn in my buckaroo string, putting them on a little outfit afterward, and then having them last another 10 years doing the work. I've shown a few horses into their late twenties and had one that was still turning cows down the fence at 32 years of age.

This longevity comes from a good gene pool, physical development of the body and the ability to move in balance—whatever is asked of the horse. These two qualities, along with complete understanding by the horse of the movements asked of him, leads to a stress-free mind. As has been said by others, the mind has to be right for the body to be right. Invariably you have to work through the body to get the mind right.

Part of maintaining a good mental attitude in your horse is that he keeps improving. You have spent six-to-eight years or longer getting your horse straight in the bridle. Having done that, the big work is done and the improvement will now come from little things that you do with your body signals and hand signals. Offer him less signal and keep expecting him to answer with quicker response.

You know each other well, so keep developing this relationship. Look for those days when you think it and the horse responds; they can, and it will happen. Watch for your horse to understand his different jobs better and make a change in his frame on his own to get there a step quicker.

The horse is balanced over his hocks and turning over his right pivot foot. He is on time with the heifer.

The horse is positioned on the cow to force a stop. This is learned behavior by the horse. You teach them what they need to know to do their job. In time, if it has been done correctly, you can do the work in one hand.

Straight in the bridle on a soft rein. This horse knows his job.

If I ride a horse in the spade bit straight up in the bridle, I will watch for him to seek self-carriage more and more. The horse has already found it in the hackamore and will hunt it again in the bridle, especially with the higher port bits. Some horses seek it right away and others need a year straight in the bridle before finding it again.

The horse will start to seek it on his own as you move him forward. As his face comes toward the vertical, there will be a point where there is no bit weight in his mouth. The bit weight is hanging from the poll of his head as he supports it with his tongue and you are supporting through the reins. Once he has found this self-carriage and it has developed a little, there are some things to do to promote it to happen more often.

I will change the bridle bit (usually the spade) to one with cheeks made with more weight, being constructed of thicker metal, but with the same mouthpiece. This extra weight, ounces different from the other bit, will cause him to hunt the position with his face so there is no weight in his mouth. This helps to create the elegant look of a bridle horse moving forward on a passive rein with frame in his top line and lifting energy in his gait.

In making a change of bridle bits with a horse, I try to gain a little nuance of difference, either in the carriage of the horse or in the quickness to respond to the signals. I have believed for years that if I got my horse straight up in the spade bit, and understanding of the signal before leverage, that he would be the quickest and the lightest in my hands.

If the bridle teeth (canine teeth) were far enough up in the upper hard palate to interfere with the spade bit and I had to bridle him with one of the other ports that would signal, I always kind of believed that I had obtained all of the potential that was there.

A Great Horse Named Bucket

I had a friend who lived with my wife and I when my boys were very young. He was becoming a very good horseman and was also a bit and spur maker. He is a perfectionist who worked hard to master both crafts. A few years later, when he was running a ranch in Nevada, he called me one night and told me his bridle horse had been hurt and would need at least six months to heal. He asked if I had a broke horse I could lend him as all his other horses were pretty green. I respected this man. I was not afraid for him to ride any of my horses.

I told him I would send him a horse named Bucket who was a straight up spade bit bridle horse. Bucket could do it all well and I think was the fastest horse I ever rode in my life. I told him to keep him as long as he needed. I was in good shape for horses.

After he had Bucket for a while, Dan called me and asked if he could try some other bridle bits on Bucket to get a feel for them. I told him he could ride him in anything he wanted. Around three weeks later, Dan called again and told me he had found a bit that Bucket was faster in. Dan was using a traditional half-breed port with Las Cruces cheeks.

Bucket had an average tongue for thickness and a tented hard palate. I had been using a Spanish-style spade with a narrow top. I told Dan that his saying the horse could be even faster was a little hard to believe and he was probably experiencing bit change phenomenon. A lot of times, when you change a bridle bit in a horse's mouth, you will get quicker response to signals with less movement and pressure. But in a ride or two, things will level out and the true reaction and response to the bridle bit will be there for you to see and feel. He said he really thought it was there. So we agreed that he would continue on and see what developed.

Two months later we talked and Dan said he still was faster in the half-breed with the Las Cruces cheeks than the Spanish Spade with Santa Barbara cheeks.

Dan is a good hand and I knew if he was saying this, he felt it to be true. I told Dan that I needed to ride Bucket to feel this, and that I didn't think it could better than when a horse was answering off a signal with a spade bit with a straight cheek.

It was quite a while before I could get to Dan's ranch to ride Bucket. However, when I did, I found that Bucket was faster in his responses to the signal. He was a real nice, fast horse in the spade bit. I thought it was as good as it was going to get. My thinking was wrong.

With the half-breed and Las Cruces cheeks, it was even better. From that experience, I have changed my thinking. I now believe that very possibly you are not going to find the ultimate bit for a particular horse. Most bridle horsemen don't have a large enough bit selection to keep trying bridle bits until they find the ultimate bit to fit their particular horse's mouth and personality.

It was an eye-opening experience for me that led me to some bit changing with my bridle horses after they were straight in the bridle in an attempt to find the ultimate bit to bring our communication with each other to a higher level. Most of the time I don't find a bridle bit faster for the horse than the spade bit with Santa Barbara cheeks.

If you try a new bridle bit, you need to use it for at least five rides to get a true feeling from the horse. If you choose to try it, it can become part of "polishing the stone."

Reaching the Highest Level

As the years go by, your horse will reach a point where he has attained his highest level of strength and quickness. It can vary a few years from horse-to-horse. When this actually happens depends upon the gene pool he came from (his dam and sire) and on how complete his gymnastic training has been. Did he have constant and correct care of his feet for the work he is doing and the least amount of mental stress that he has to deal with to live in our world? Remember that he is not here by his choice. He is here by our choice.

When that day does come, and he is starting down the other side of the mountain, recognize it for what it is. A slight loss of quickness in movements…he can't quite handle the real heavy cattle on the end of a rope the way he used to…the long days and miles that now require more days of recovery before the next turn….

He is not done, just slowing down, and if I will give him some consideration for this, he can last another five-to-seven years before going into retirement when the kids are going to get to ride him. Give him the easier work and no more pounding the rocks.

The training of the California-Style Vaquero Bridle Horse, if done correctly, is an art form. It creates great fluidity of motion and complete harmony between horse and rider. Unfortunately, however, it is not an art form that endures like a painting or sculpture. It remains a life which ends when the two of you part, by passing the horse on to someone else or by the death of the horse.

For me, this parting can be very emotional, like losing a friend and teacher who I trusted and who trusted me in return. Yet the memories remain and give solace. And the journey continues….

Glossary

Aligning the Structures - Preparing the horse's body correctly to do a movement.

Arc Turnaround - A 360-degree turn with bend in the horse's body.

Balance - Ability in the horse to be in the correct alignment in any movement with equilibrium.

Balance-in-Arc - Equilibrium maintained while the horse has bend in his body.

Bend - To have contraction on one side of the horse and lengthening the other side.

Bosal - Also referred to as a Jaquima. Traditionally, it consists of braided rawhide around a core of more rawhide. There is a nose-button on the front, two side-buttons and a heel knot. The egg-shaped loop goes over the horses nose. Part of a hackamore.

Brace - The resistance in muscles in the horse that retards fluid motion when we ask the horse to move different body parts.

Bridle Box - An area in front of the fork on the saddle above the neck of the horse approximately 11 inches long and seven inches wide, $3^{1/2}$ inches on either side of the horse's mane. The bridle reins need to stay to in this box to keep the bridle bit from tilting in the horse's mouth.

Bump - A lateral (sideways) not backward movement of the hand (in a horizontal position with the knuckles up), coming from the wrist not the arm so as to rotate the nose button of the hackamore causing the horse's face to move toward the vertical.

California hanger - a metal piece put on the end of the headstall with a very thin metal strap that goes through the bit hanger holes.

Cant or Canted - Angular deviation from a vertical or horizontal plane.

Canter - A three-beat gait, with a moment of suspension, while maintaining contact with the horse's face.

Closed Back - When the spinous processes of the vertebra are pushed closer to each other, you'd refer to this as a closed back. This happens when the back is in a concave position and the base of the neck is pushed down.

Colt - Any horse, regardless of age, just starting into training.

Come To My Hands - A change in the horse's neck and face toward vertical, caused by engagement of the hip, or a shortening of the reins, or both.

Curve Groove of the Lip - Where the upper and lower lips join.

Diagonal Balance - In the horse; equilibrium is maintained from left hip through the right shoulder, or the right hip through the left shoulder, depending upon which lead the horse is on.

Drive - Traction from the stroke of the horse's legs.

Energy - The power of the movement

Face - Position of the horse's face from contact with the rider's hands.

Feathering the rein - Raising and lowering the rein next to the horse's neck to accentuate the movement of the horse's shoulder.

Finished - Straight up in the bridle.

Fixed Hand - A rein position applied to the face of the horse and fixed solid (tied) to some part of the rigging the horse is wearing around it's mid-body. Example, saddle or surcingle.

Flexion - Bend or arching of the horse's body.

Forward - The end result of drive. It is the horse moving straight with energy in a specific direction with rein contact to the face and influence to different structures in his body.

Fluidness, Fluidity - Graceful movement.

Frame - Any change in the horse's body toward collection.

A Gather - To collect cattle to a given spot.

"Going down the fence" - To control a cow next to a fence or barrier by driving and holding it to the fence or barrier, stopping and turning it back the other direction.

Gymnastication - Developing strength and agility.

Hackamore - Made up of three things; a bosal, mecáte and lightweight hanger.

Hip-in, travers - A gymnastic move where the horse's hip is displaced to the inside of the line of travel.

Home Base - Where all hand signals should start from and where the hands should be when riding. It is the area right in front of the fork of the saddle and two to three inches above the horse's mane.

"Horse in my Hands", "In my hands" - The same as "come to my hands."

Lass Rope - A rope to catch cattle or horses.

Lifting Energy - The energy created by the horse's legs during movement when it's back is open or arched.

Lope - A three-beat gait with a moment of suspension with no contact with the horse's face.

Mecáte, McCarty - Reins used with a bosal; usually made of hair; part of the hackamore.

Obliques - Muscle group on the side of the horse's barrel (mid-section).

Open Back - When the horse's back is arched and the thoracic vertebrae have extended upwards. Like the opening of a fan.

Over-flexing - When the outside eye passes the inside point of the opposite shoulder.

Passive Contact - A slight drape in the reins but still short enough to maintain feel of the horse's mouth. When using the hackamore it means that you can feel the bosal but you are not influencing the horse's face.

Passive Rein - A long rein with contact with the horse's mouth. When using the hackamore, it means no signal to the horse but some contact with the bosal.

Purist - Adhering only to one discipline, not mixing other ideas or movements.

Reata - Rawhide braided rope used to rope cattle or horses (lass rope).

Resistance - Any force that tends to oppose or retard motion.

Roll Back - 180 degree turn that is started when the horse is in the last phase of a stop, and before all the energy of the stop has left the body of the horse.

Rodear - An open area where the cattle to be worked are held by a group of riders in a circle around them.

Self-carriage - Change in the frame of the horse that is created by the horse himself without having the horse in hand. The horse changes the position of his neck, poll and face to open his withers on his own. The horse creates a longer top-line and a shorter base.

Shoulder-in - A gymnastic move where the horse's shoulder is displaced to the inside of the line of travel.

Stop - A movement that is created at the end of the motion.

Straight - Extending continuously in the same direction.

Straight-up Bridle Horse - A horse being ridden with a bridle bit only.

Straight-Bridled - A horse put into the bridle without the use of the two-rein set up.

Sweet Spot - Place on the nose of the horse where he reacts the fastest to the signals from the hackamore.

Thrusting Energy - Traction and drive produced by the legs of the horse that propels his body forward with power.

Transitioning rotation - The fulcrum point from the canon in the horses mouth that creates energy up and forward in arc and then back toward the chinstrap.

Traditionalist - One who uses any time-honored set of practices.

Tug - A lateral movement of the forearm of the rein hand with no break in the wrist and with the hand out in a slightly knuckle-up position to bring more of the bar of the hackamore into the face or into the jawbone of the horse.

Long Lines - Two long reins that allow you to manipulate and control the body of the horse from a distance.

"Wadded up" - When the horse's body is tight or when he doesn't want to move.

"Whooie" Knot - A knot used when tying the reins on to a bosal (half-hitch).

Expanded Table of Contents

Chapter 1 – Early Training ~ 1

How Horses Think 1
What is a Colt? 1
The Round Pen 2
    Difference Between Lope and Canter 2
Balance in Arc 2
    Closed Back 3
Developing Understanding 3
Mental Yielding 4
Hindquarters 4
Testing Your Program 5
Forequarters 5
Moving the Jaw and Atlas 6
Work Ethic and Patience 7
Lass Rope Work 11
The First Saddling 13
Forward to the Back-Up 14
Think Time 14
Light Fixed Hand 16
    The 14th Thoracic Vertebrae 16
    What is Fixed Hands 17
Biomechanics of Fixed Hands 17
Use of the Single Pillar or Circus Pole 18
Placement of the Pole 18
    Different Kinds of Circus Poles 20
Patterning the Horse on the Pole 20
What to Look For 22
Reaching the Goal of the Pole 23
    Use of Whips and Sticks 23
Changes in the Horse 23
Signals and Positions at the Pole 24
The First Ride 24
Human Riding Influence 25

Italic emphasis indicates information in sideboxes
All other items are subheads or text content

CHAPTER 2 - THE HACKAMORE AS A DISCIPLINE ~ 27

Design of the Bosal 27
Mechanics of the Bosal 29
    Notes on the Hackamore 29
The Heel Knot 30
Hackamore Reins.. 31
Bosal and Rein Changes to Build a True Hackamore Horse 32
Knowing When to Change 33
    Bosal and Rope Changes Chart 33
Finish Work 34
Finding Release from Pressure 35
    Hand Positions for the Hackamore 35
Speed of Signals 36
    Bosal Length and Number of Mecáte Wraps 36
Tying the Reins to the Bosal 37

CHAPTER 3 - INTRODUCING THE HACKAMORE TO THE YOUNG HORSE ~ 43

The Sweet Spot 43
Bald Spots.. 43
Placement of Bosal on the Nose 43
Pre-Ride Hackamore Ground Work... 44
First Ride in the Hackamore 46
Forward on a Supporting Rein... 46
Home Base 47
Social Braces and Training Braces... 48
Coming to Vertical 48
    Shortening the Base 49
    Feathers, Wood, Iron 50
Coming Vertical and Lateral Flexion.. 51
    What is Lateral Flexion?.. 52
Teach at the Walk, School at the Trot... 55

Chapter 4 - Development Work in the Hackamore: The Exercises ~57

- Riding Inside and Outside 57
  - *The Use and Size of Circles* 57
- Developing Body Strength in the Young Horse 58
- The Start of Lope Work 58
  - *The Difference Between the Lope and the Canter* 58
- The Start of Transition Work 61
- Aligning the Structures 61
- Canter Work on a Circle 62
- Suppling and Strengthening Exercises 63
- Riding a Straight Line 63
- The Leg Yield 64
- The Shoulder-Fore and the Shoulder-In 66
- The Circus Pole 67
- Looking for Good Effort 68
- Changing Directions on the Pole 68
- Biomechanics of the Turn 68
- The Side Pass 69
- Travers and the Hip-In 70
- Signals for the Horse 71
- Developing Forward in the Horse 72
- Thrusting Leg, Lifting Leg 73
- Developing the Stop 73
- Signals for the Stop 74
- The Back-Up 75
- Speed to the Back-Up 76
- Turn on the Forehand 76
- Turn on the Hips 77
- The Turnaround 78
- Signals for the Turnaround 79
- A Note from Frank Barnett on Turnaround Timing 80
- Moving Laterally 81
- Suppling and Gymnastic Exercises 81
- Shoulder-In to a Leg Yield 82
- Leg Yield to Leg Yield 82
- Leg Yield to a Counter Arc, Half Circle, Back to Leg Yield 83
- Quarter Turns and Half Turns 83

Chapter 5 - Introducing Cattle Work and Roping ~ 85

Mental Confidence and Understanding 86
Positions in Relation to the Cow... 86
Rodear Work 87
Corral Work 88
Up to this Point 90
Incorrect Rider Body and Hand Positions.. 91
Correct Rider Body and Hand Positions 92
Building Distance, Improving Movements... 93
Introduction to Roping Cattle 94
At the Branding Pen 97

Chapter 6 - Riding with the Snaffle Bit ~ 99

My Early Experiences.. 99
Tips from Experienced Hands 100
Using the Snaffle Today 100

Chapter 7 - Intermediate Hackamore Work ~ 103

Developing Self Carriage 103
What is Self Carriage?.. 103
Riding My String... 103
Challenging your Horse 104
Higher Levels of Balance 105
The Post Pen (Square Pen) 106
Post Pen Historical Notes... 106
Circling the Pole in the Post Pen 108
More Demanding Suppling and Gymnastic Work 112
Size of the Round Pen 113
Intensifying the Cow Work... 114
Rating the Cow's Speed... 116
The Test of Speed 117
The Cow's Pressure Zones 118

Chapter 8 - Finish Work in the Hackamore ~ 119

Speed of the Signals 119
Rein Influences 121
The Finished Product.. 122

Chapter 9 - The Two-Rein Bosal ~ How it Works ~ 123

Adding Hand Signals.. 124

CHAPTER 10 - THE HORSE'S MOUTH ~ 127

Teeth and Dental Care 127
Examining the Mouth and It's Parts 128

CHAPTER 11 - VAQUERO-STYLE BRIDLE BITS ~ 131

Lasting History 131
How the Bit Works 131
The True Mechanics of the Bridle Bit 132
Development of the Signal Bit 134
Pictures and Descriptions of Bridle Bits 135

CHAPTER 12 - IS MY HORSE READY FOR THE BRIDLING PROCESS? ~ 145

CHAPTER 13 - STARTING THE HORSE IN THE TWO-REIN ~ 147

Using What You Have 147
Experimenting with Bits 148
Creating Leverage with the Chinstrap 149
Romal Reins 150
Putting it On 150
Hand Influences on the Reins 151
Hand Positions 152
Signs of Progress to Look For 158

CHAPTER 14 - RIDING THE HORSE STRAIGHT IN THE BRIDLE ~ 161

Knowing When He's Ready 161
Horses I've Bridled 162
Odd Things Happen 163
How to Hold the Reins 164
Being Straight Up in the Bridle 167

CHAPTER 15 - POLISHING THE STONE ~ 169

Horse Longevity 169
A Great Horse Named Bucket 171
Reaching the Highest Level 172
The Journey Continues 172

About the Author

Mike Bridges was born in Southern California in 1940. He is an internationally known clinician and bridle horseman in the California Vaquero Style with more than fifty five years of making his living on the back of a horse.

He began learning the Vaquero tradition as a teenager from his grandfather who advised him to seek out other vaqueros to deepen his knowledge. Mike left home at the age of 15 to buckaroo on various ranches in California and Nevada where he learned from those who lived this old tradition. Today he is one of the few who can still build a traditional California Vaquero "turn at the touch" Bridle Horse.

The California Vaquero Style can be traced to the style of riding brought to Mexico and Southern California from the Iberian peninsula by the Portuguese and Spanish Conquistadors who explored these new worlds. It is this link to the Portuguese and Spanish Conquistador that resulted in the similarities in horsemanship of the California Vaquero, the Doma Vaquera of the Iberian peninsula and the French School of Classical Riding.

Notes